By George F. Butterick

Editor

Poetry and Truth by Charles Olson (1970)
Additional Prose by Charles Olson (1974)
The Maximus Poems: Volume Three by Charles Olson, with
    Charles Boer (1975)
Selected Poems by Vincent Ferrini (1976)
Muthologos: The Collected Lectures and Interviews by
    Charles Olson (1978-79)
The Postmoderns: The New American Poetry Revised, with
    Donald Allen (1980)
*Charles Olson & Robert Creeley: The Complete Correspondence
    Volumes 1 & 2* (1980)

Author

The Norse (1973)
Reading Genesis by the Light of a Comet (1976)
A Guide to the Maximus Poems of Charles Olson (1978)

Journal

OLSON: The Journal of the Charles Olson Archives (1974-78)

CHARLES OLSON & ROBERT CREELEY:

THE COMPLETE
CORRESPONDENCE
VOLUME I
EDITED BY
GEORGE F. BUTTERICK

BLACK SPARROW PRESS
SANTA BARBARA   1980

ACKNOWLEDGEMENT

Robert Creeley's poems "Still Life Or" and "The Epic Expands" have been collected in *The Charm: Early and Uncollected Poems*, published by the Four Seasons Foundation as part of its Writing series in 1969.

Cover photographs by Gerard Malanga.

LIBRARY OF CONGRESS CATALOGING IN PUBLICATION DATA

Olson, Charles, 1910-1970.
    Charles Olson & Robert Creeley.

    Includes index.
    1. Olson, Charles, 1910-1970—Correspondence.   2. Creeley, Robert, 1926-   —Correspondence.   3. Poets, American—20th century—Correspondence.   I. Creeley, Robert, 1926-   II. Butterick, George F. III. Title.
PS3529.L655Z544   811'.54   80-12222
ISBN 0-87685-400-5 (v. 1)
ISBN 0-87685-401-3 (deluxe : v. 1)
ISBN 0-87685-399-8 (pbk. : v. 1)

ACKNOWLEDGEMENTS

The originals of Robert Creeley's letters to Charles Olson are among the Olson papers in the Literary Archives, University of Connecticut Library, and are published here with the library's kind permission. Charles Olson's original letters to Robert Creeley are primarily—with the exceptions noted in the copyright statement earlier—among Creeley's papers on deposit at Washington University Library, St. Louis, and are included here with that library's kind cooperation. Photographs of Robert Creeley, his letters to Olson, and Olson's 23 June 1950 letter to him, were generously made available by the University of Connecticut Library and are used here with permission. The photograph of Olson with his wife Constance in Washington, spring 1950, is by Marc Riboud and was made available courtesy of his brother, Jean Riboud. Creeley's letters to Jacob R. Leed quoted in my notes are also in the Literary Archives at the University of Connecticut Library.

Acknowledgement must be made above all to Donald Allen for friendly wisdom and for providing typescripts and photocopies of most of Olson's letters, and for otherwise advancing this project. Holly Hall, head of Rare Books and Special Collections at Washington University Libraries, graciously supplied photocopies of additional Olson letters among the materials under her charge. My students Hedda Friberg and John Morgan provided valuable assistance in preparing the notes, and Seamus Cooney, who prepared the index, also gave very sound advice on preparing the final manuscript for the printer.

G. F. B.

TABLE OF CONTENTS

Editor's Introduction

As early as August 2 of 1950, less than four months into their correspondence, Charles Olson was aware of the significance of his writing
to Robert Creeley. He wrote to his old friend and fellow Melvillean,
Henry A. Murray: "Creeley and I have since engaged in perhaps the
most important correspondence of my life." It is as a result of this
correspondence—and also the possibilities Creeley offered as publisher
and editor—that Olson will term him "The Figure of Outward" in his
1960 dedication to *The Maximus Poems;* while within that series itself,
Creeley is handsomely acknowledged by Olson as having given him
what he calls "the world." What he actually meant by those terms is
summarized by Olson in a note to himself near the end of his life:

> the Figure of Outward means way out way out
> *there:* the
> 'World,' I'm sure, otherwise
> why was the pt. then to like write to Creeley
> daily? to make that whole thing
> double, to
> objectify the extension of an
> 'outward'? a[n] opposite to a
> personality which so completely does (did)
> stay at home?

Creeley, in his turn, who had known the best the American university
had to offer, dropping out of Harvard in his final year, found Olson's
letters "of such energy and calculation that they constituted a practical
'college' of stimulus and information." Elsewhere he writes: "The letters . . . were really my education just because their range and articu-
lation took me into terms of writing and many other areas indeed
where I otherwise might never have entered." One can expect to find,
then, in the letters that follow, a relationship and a correspondence of
uncommon richness.

The occasion of the initial letter can be quickly told. In March
1950, Olson sent a few poems to Vincent Ferrini, whom he had sought
out in Gloucester the previous year. They were offered as a gesture of

friendship as well as some indication of the direction of his writing. Ferrini liked the poems well enough and sent two of them in additon to some of his own to Creeley, who had written from New Hampshire that he was planning a literary magazine that promised to be "free of the current impositions of the literary hierarchy." The two Olson poems were "Lost Aboard U. S. S. 'Growler,'" a retitling of "Pacific Lament," which had been written in 1945 as a tribute to a friend drowned in wartime submarine service, and "The Laughing Ones," alternatively titled "Otvechai" (Russian imperative, "Answer!"). One of Olson's earliest poems, "Lost Aboard" had already been published in the *Atlantic Monthly*, while "The Laughing Ones" again was not new, but written the previous November as part of a letter to Edward Dahlberg. It was Creeley's less than favorable response to these specific poems, reported directly by Ferrini—along with a suggestion that had just come in the morning's mail from William Carlos Williams—that caused Olson to write the first letter that launched one of the most important relationships of recent literary history.

The correspondence begins at a time before Olson had completed his famous "Projective Verse" essay (revised in the course of these early letters) and before the first *Maximus* poem was written, with only *Call Me Ishmael* and "The Kingfishers" any indication of the power and scope of his drive. He would write his first *Maximus* poem as a letter to Vincent Ferrini in a few weeks and hit stride with "In Cold Hell, In Thicket," also written that May. Creeley, on the other hand—at least at the start of the correspondence—is primarily a story writer, seeking to be a man of letters, having found directions for a literary life in Pound and Williams. As a poet, he has read Hart Crane, Cummings, and Patchen, and found Wallace Stevens of special value. As a result of the exchange with Olson, he will write "Hart Crane" and "Le Fou" and step into rhythms in his poetry more associated with his actual life. The rise of both men to their full powers is directly observable in the letters to come.

There are roughly one thousand surviving pieces of correspondence in all, with Creeley outwriting Olson at a rate of three to one. Because of the intensity and totality of the engagement, the decision was made not to reduce them to a single-volume selection, but to publish them at full length, in several successive volumes. When the series is finally complete, it will be seen that the letters extend from April of 1950 to January 1, 1970, only days before Olson's death. They diminish in frequency and size on both sides during the later years, but nevertheless remain full of interest. Indeed, they are not only endlessly fascinating as human documents, the very real lives of very deliberate minds, but they are equally rewarding for their history of the era. The early letters, especially—and certainly those through 1954—stand together as a critical document for understanding the emerging poetics of a generation, as well as, perhaps, of the poetries yet to come.

The letters include discussions of poems under hand, the first tentative or bold showings of those writings (some published here for the first time), the exchange of insight and judgment, strategies of publishing, personal history, comments on predecessors and reactions to contemporaries, eager embracings, cautions, scorns. Each man allowed the other his head, took what came, and found of interest (or at least discussible) each other's preoccupations. Sometimes a dialogue ensued, other times one generously allowed himself to be used as a sounding board for the other's necessities. Together they hammered out a poetics—both the specialized craft of the wordsmith, but also the larger issue of how a man of language must live in the world.

The first volume concludes at a point where Olson's "Projective Verse," revised as a result of the exchange with Creeley, is about to emerge; while the entire first year's worth of letters, those from 1950, will end with the Olsons about to depart for the Yucatan, with Creeley wishing them well (although the sudden death of Olson's mother on Christmas Day will intervene, postponing the trip a few weeks). From this trip result the letters Creeley edited and published as Olson's *Mayan Letters*, although the unabridged texts will be made available in this series for the first time.

Olson's letters, at least in the early years, are most often typewritten; Creeley's almost always so—with remarkably few typing errors—despite the fact he is a self-confessed bidigital typist. They are often double-spaced, although he increasingly moves to single-space as the correspondence progresses and especially after his move to France and Mallorca, where paper and airmail postage were at a premium. No distinction has been made, in such a "reader's edition" as this, as to whether a letter was originally handwritten or a typescript. Post cards, similarly, are not distinguished from letters proper. Some of Olson's early letters were lost in Creeley's moves during those years—from New Hampshire to France, from France to Mallorca, and back to this country in 1954, with no permanent storage place until he was to buy a house in Placitas, New Mexico, in 1963. Some of Creeley's letters from early 1951 got water-damaged while being stored by Olson and have proved thus far irretrievable. So gaps occasionally appear in the exchange—a major one (on Olson's side) between 31 July 1950 and the end of that year (that will be more than made up for in future volumes). Moreover, in that case, Creeley's letters in themselves remain thoroughly engaging, and it is possible for the reader to imaginatively supply most of the context.

A few words on editing practices used in the presentation of these letters are appropriate. The task of the editor throughout has been to offer a readable yet faithful text. The letters published here are intended to be exact transcriptions of the originals. Every effort has been made to observe their original forms. The most difficult aspect to reproduce or transpose, metamorphose—almost in an Ovidian sense—from typewritten or holograph original into printer's type, was, as always, the spacing of the letters. To begin, headings have been standardized only to the extent that they appear flush right, with places and dates supplied when necessary, always within square brackets. Paragraphing and indentation have been followed as closely as possible. Indentations are generally given as they occur in the originals, although occasionally a more standard indentation has been assigned, where such regularization would not betray the author's purpose or emphasis. Original line lengths and breaks are preserved where a particular effect, such as a conscious syncopation, is sought. For purposes of economy—both visual, and printing costs—excessive or multiple spacings between lines have not always been observed, especially where some original letters have been typed double-spaced. Occasionally a letter will break into line arrangements which are more familiarly those of a poem; indeed, such letters, by compression and force of language, may be nothing *but* poems.

Afterthoughts inserted by the authors in margins have been indicated as such, within brackets in the course of the text, even though such impede ever so slightly the flow of the letter. This was thought to be more faithful to the original moment of composition as well as to the recipient's first reading of the letter. Similarly, although footnote numbers have been inserted throughout the text, the notes themselves have been gathered at the back—once again because the live text is paramount. Corrections made by the authors above words or lines have usually been incorporated directly and silently in the flow of text. Only significant alterations by the authors or uncertain readings by the editor are reported otherwise (within square brackets). When added material appears on the top of the first page of a letter, after the body of the letter had been typed—a common Creeley practice—it is presented at the *end* of the published letter, with its original location identified, to avoid confusion.

I have silently corrected certain occasional errors, usually typographical in nature, or misspellings. Every author has three or four unshakeable, irremediable ones. Olson, for example, consistently misspelled "millennia" with a single *n*, and in his haste with the typewriter had several spellings for "rhythm." I have not, however, otherwise revised or "improved" the text.

I have been especially cautious in matters of spelling and abbreviations, since it is never clear when a pun might suddenly arise (or descend). One particularly troublesome spot will serve as example, where Olson, in writing about Ezra Pound (in his 9 June 1950 letter), rather than using the familiar "Ez," seems to dismiss his former mentor, the once great poet, as "Ex." A pun, one that Olson in his annoyance with Pound was capable of, or a typing error, the X and Z being so close to each other on the keyboard? I have left it up to the reader to decide.

On occasion punctuation has been added, such as a period at the end of a postscript or a closing parenthesis, where consistency and sense clearly demand it. I have been all the while cognizant, however, of Olson's use of such a thing as the open parenthesis as a structural device, or, even more, part of a *theme* of openness, as when he writes in "La Préface":

> Draw it thus: (   ) 1910 (
> It is not obscure. We are the new born, and there are no
> flowers.
>
> Document means there are no flowers
>
> and no parenthesis

—the significance of which Creeley immediately recognizes in the early letters—or Creeley's own use of the device in such early poems as "Le Fou" or "A Song."

Unlike in the cases of some of the notable editing projects of recent times, such as Larabee's *Papers of Benjamin Franklin* or Syrett's *Papers of Alexander Hamilton*, what may appear to be superfluous punctuation, especially commas, on the part of both authors, has not been removed. The nuances gained by commas, dashes, colons, are the same nuances and multiplicity of meanings that are gained by careful line breaks and punctuation in a typical Creeley or Olson poem. In both cases in this mutually supportive correspondence, the sentences of each author conform meticulously, almost phrenologically, to the contours of the authors' thought. Their thought takes shape, has discernible pattern—down to the exasperations, the enthusiasms, the outrages and speculations, the racing wit. It is part of the confidence of their particular genius. Olson was excited even while dying that there might be a machine (in his case a hospital spectroscope) to measure his body in language, to print or bespeak his soul. And isn't his hope for the typewriter in "Projective Verse" simply a faith in language as a pattern we can all participate in?

Some of the idiosyncratic usages and proliferation of commas may be initially distracting. One might suggest that both men are, at the beginning—just as Creeley in his letter to Ferrini first accused Olson of doing—"looking for a language," seeking to avoid the routine and mannered language of both predecessors and the majority of contemporaries. But it would be wrong to consider theirs primarily a language of defiance and resistance, sign and countersign between only themselves. Creeley keenly participated in the rhythms of the new speech that issued parallel to jazz, and while Olson had relatively little experience of jazz (limited, perhaps, to Fats Waller and the stride and boogie-woogie pianos of Greenwich Village Café Society days of the late thirties), he trusted his American speech in whatever forms he heard it, and was certainly alive to rhythm—in language, in his walk, in gestures. Mostly it is an *animated* conversation these men are engaged in—somewhat desperately at times, in their own chosen, relative isolation—Creeley with his young family on a New Hampshire farm, and later in southern France and Mallorca; Olson in his snug (at times

xiv

cramped) Washington studio, then in Yucatan and at Black Mountain. They are working out a place for themselves at the frontiers of world writing, cut off by indifference and entrenched interests, seeking to communicate from their respective foxholes. It is possible to think of them at the start, awaiting each other's voice (Olson called Creeley from a pay phone just before leaving for the Yucatan to hear what he sounded like), imagining what one another *looked* like (there is an exchange of photographs), Olson estimating with his wife Creeley's age. (They were a bit off. In the same letter to Harry Murray quoted from earlier, Olson writes, "I have, by the way, no guess on how old Creeley is: Connie and I debate it daily! The best guess, c 30!") Creeley was twenty-three at the time, Olson thirty-nine; they were not to meet in person for almost four years, until March 1954, when Creeley arrived to teach at Black Mountain College. It was almost the same difference in age as Hawthorne and Melville (only reversed), a fact perhaps not lost on Olson.

But it would be better not to attempt to provide too complete a background for each writer here; rather, let the writers' lives and circumstances unfold for the reader just as they revealed themselves to each other. At times it seems they wrote not to entertain, or even instruct, but to survive.

George F. Butterick

Charles Olson & Robert Creeley:
The Complete Correspondence

Volume 1

Notes to the letters begin on p. 159.

my dear robert creeley:

so Bill W[illiams] too sez, write creeley, he
has ideas and wants to USE 'em

so what do i do?   so i write   so ferrini sends
creeley a lovely liquid thing, and creeley says, he's a boll weevil, olson,
just a lookin' for a lang, just a lookin   nuts, and
i says, creeley, you're
off yr trolley: a man
god damn well has to come up with his own lang., syntax and song both,
but also each poem under hand has its own language, which is variant of
same ((THIS IS THE BATTLE: i wish very much, creeley, i had now to
        send you what PNY publishes summer issue, *PROjective Verse
        vs. the NON-projective:*[1] the argument pitches here
                                                    (I've
        dubbed the alternative to composing by inherited forms
        "composition by field"—it needs more examination than I give
        it, in that kick-off piece))

did that Twin of mine (he's, in Gloucester, the
Poet; I, there, where i grew up, am ex-letter carrier, ex-fisherman,
ex-character; so it does my soul no end of beauty to have vinc. making
with the woids)
                    did he shoot along to you ASYMPTOTES? he sd he
was figurin to
                    i got a big rough baby THE MORNING NEWS
which may bounce off its first stop   if it does, i'll toss it to you   but there
is the enclosed 1st child of new england which i am soft about, and send
for yr lookin'

also, this copyright edition of *y & x* (it layed an
egg a yr ago in a subscriber first, designed differently, and much larger:
Preface suffers from the photo-shrink

hello, this is,
direct,

                                        Olson

[*Added in ink:*]
& *La Chute*

                                Littleton, N.H.
                                April 24, 1950

Dear Olsen,

Have your poems at hand. These are too much—unlike what I had seen; forgive, etc. But the others didn't make it for me, and, perhaps, useless to go into that here. Except to say that you have my vote on the matters of language, etc. It was, in those, that I couldn't come to it, etc., but as you will.

So will print MORNING NEWS in this first issue; and will keep, if you will, the others to look at for a subsequent one. I w'd say that MOVE OVER w'd be it, for something later; but will write you on this, when I can come to it.

Good that the Dr. took the trouble to say those things, etc. This means much. I.e., more than goodwill, some help. Very few can make this. Anyhow, I'll make use of his 'program' and also, by the way of emphasis, a reprint of his article on Eliot in the Feb '48 issue of 4 Pages.[2] Do you know this? Expect you w'd. At the moment, have a rather tenuous relation with same, via so many, that I can only shout, etc. But for one: T. D. Horton has been of great help in these matters; through him, some fine things by Paquette, which will also make use of in this first issue.[3] But you will see. It comes, at times, to making peace among these various, but granted the will, perhaps (dare we hope) the way, etc. So much for that.

I saw ASYMPTOTES, and have to say I'm happy with what I've got. Again, forgive, etc. You will know how we are about these things.

To each his own, etc.

Very grateful for the copy of Y&X; the first thing very, very good. You'll have to take it, that lacking this kind of substance, or better, not knowing about it, the first poems I saw suffered, accordingly. Not to back down on that matter—NEVER. But this much to say how much I like what I find here.

Anyhow, send some more of these fine things, whenever you have them to spare. Also: when you want to come to these matters in prose, send that too. Always room, or will make it, for these things.

Best to you,

Robert Creeley

Nota: I am still laughing, like they say. I hope people can pick up on this thing (MORNING NEWS). I think, with horror, of those who are not amused, etc. This, in any event, saves me a lot of wind, etc. Thanks.

———

[Littleton, N.H.]
Apr/28/50

Dear Olson,

This is redundant, etc. But these past few days, have been looking at the poems in the little book, staring. Very, very good of you to have sent it. When loot, etc., allows, will ask for a few copies to send to those who are still looking for something like this. What can I say: I take you to put down here movement beyond what the Dr., Stevens, etc., have made for us. Wonderful things.

Have taken the liberty of making a short note on these things for the magazine; together with one on Crews[4] who is dead, somewhat, in the head, but no matter. It's yourself I'm concerned with. Because of space, etc., not much chance to say more than LOOK AT THIS, but that's part of it. For the note: quote some of La Preface & The Green Man. Now, I wd take parts of The Moebus Strip to be it, but again I take La Preface to show something the deadheads never thought of, and/or, the 'simple' condensation of WHAT'S HAPPENED. And/or 'not only "comment" but container.' The compression, without DISTORTION, in this thing: too much. And through all of this, you make your own rhythms, language, always the POEM. With all the deadwood around, & all the would-be 'form,' etc., I take these things as coming head-on.

Thinking of Stevens, who slipped into PR, with this: 'Poetic form in its proper sense is a question of what appears within the poem itself. . . By appearance within the poem itself one means the things created and existing there. . .'[5] Basic. Yet they won't see it, that it cannot be a box or a bag or what you will. Like Eliot: the imposition of tradition etc., etc. Both senses to apply. You *cannot* put 1 tradition on top of another, without losing what APPLIES in each. . . Like these idiots who will not take what *is* of use but insist on 'returns' &tc.

Anyhow—sick at the heart.

So, then, must count on yourself to help me at times with this, by way of poetry, & criticism. A suggestion. We plan an open forum on American Universities, etc. To be, in point of fact, on *methods* of blocking what few IDEAS this country possesses, etc. False representation: beginning with when the prof said, no, that is not so, etc. etc. You must SEE it THUS, etc., etc. A matter of life *in* death, if you will. So, then, what you could bring to bear on these matters wd help. A suggestion: what we can get on this will at times be from 'names' which the 'public' takes as red, etc., so better, perhaps, to print these things anonymously, and explain: this is to avoid these preconceptions & to get to what's being discussed. The ideas, etc. But when you will. Always good to hear, so when you can. Let me know how people take the little book. Those who have eyes, etc.

Best to you,
Robert Creeley

[*Added at top of letter:*] Will plan to print the 2 other poems here in the next issue. Plans shift at the moment; I had a note from the one who'll print this he wants something to run 8-16pp to appear every two weeks. Myself, double that length, once a month. But we get to it.

[Black Mountain, N.C.]
tuesday may whatever it is
[9 May 1950]

my dear robert creeley:

      this is going to be a note, only, to tell you i have been on the road for ten days, and will write you the moment i am back at my desk

      but i want you to know how very glad i am that you saw Morning News, and that goes for y & x, and the new two, too it is fine

      it did startle me, you speak of education, & plan to speak up: nothing could be truer, when poets are the only pedagogues

      i don't think you could know that you would catch me, with yr letter, when I was at Alabama College doing a speech on verse and showing Cagli drawings And now i am here at this little hotbox of education, to do the same

      i shall try to put down something on education for you: USE, it is the use they make of us above all things resist, to be sick at heart: we are forward, and it is such gratification, that you are ready to go with me

love,
olson

[Littleton, N.H.]
Thursday
[11 May 1950]

Dear Olson,

Good to have yr letter, and good, too, mine found you where it did. So many I know are in those places now, or headed for them, because, bless us, we have to eat, etc., etc., etc. Myself, I never made the whole thing, and left 1 term short of the fatal approval. My poor mother: 20 exact yrs of saving & work, to send her lad to Hahvuhd, where the old man had went, before me, and 'its blood was green, etc., etc.' I cant face her these quiet days; we stick to our own ways. So much for the background, etc. A tear.

So, then: good to have the fact of yr interest. I trust you for something good here. To date: have word from Emerson (golden goose) that he will give something; which, depending on time, may go in this 1st issue. We lack, there, at the moment, a center, beyond the Dr.'s shot, which being a reprint, we cant bank on for applause, certainly. I have made a few things there, but I get self-conscious writing the whole thing. With good work surrounded. My boy who prints this, and who, now, takes a hand (AT LAST) cant give me an exact idea as to how often or how much we can print on the press: but we will keep to it, altho the monthly appearances may be beyond it because of the job of printing & because of distribution. Should note his comment: 'the olson being all you say it is. . . ' I sent him copies of the other two & the same with them. So, we're with you. Really fine things. Have tipped Emerson to yr little book and others I can get to: not only to fawn, etc., but, true, to see if I hold a lone opinion. I think not. Hope it gets around.

Inexperience, etc., make impossible an exact grip on the center at this writing. The Dr. said: ideas; yes, and I wd like to use them. But reading this morning in the UNWOBBLING PIVOT, like they say, a few simple precepts for SUCCESS.[6] Or notes on how to prepare for the work at hand. Neither of us have had any experience in this biz; neither of us have a clear idea, at the moment, as to what bulk or frequency we can plan. My boy does say, with truth, the best thing: to plan, say, 6 issues on one center, hit it, in good critical prose, and put the good poems & stories along with it, and no attempt to make these last fit a complex PLAN, and/or, to warp them into an ambiguous relation with the criticism. In the case of yr Morning News, its purposes fall to hand, like manna. But not usual. I dont think we can get to an exact 'program' which will embrace with sincerity the present concerns of Williams, Pound, etc., etc. In the case of the Dr.: we come close because we take him to be a focus for these matters. But always, our own way, has to be it. You will know about this, certainly. Better, to make actual limits, weedings, on what might concern us and get beyond the simple broadsheet into the kind of order that a magazine wd be, even something like PR, which otherwise I wdn't like to think about. So. This 1st issue: no articulate program beyond the airing of specific concerns, here & there, and good evidence of good poetry, etc. But we have there: no 'long-range' view. I wonder if such wd best suit our purposes at the moment. Something seems necessary & yet I hate to warp or limit what development experience might get us to. All this for what concerns me at the moment. Nothing a final block. Will write you more exact information as I have it. On the education: you can plan on this being the main concern for the next issue anyhow, and maybe for the next 2 or 3 after it. Certainly not something that can be dealt with in a few mouthfuls. Think of prose for a minute. I get scared at this point. You say the poets are the only pedagogues: whatever happened to prose . . .

Am going to ask a favor, like they say, having to do, exactly, with the

enclosed check for 60¢ which, being an honest man, I offer in payment
for 2 copies of Y&X plus mailing costs, etc. Handling, like they say.
Anyhow, wd you please send one of these to: E[leanor] BARON,
BRANDEIS UNIVERSITY, WALTHAM, MASS. It wd do her good to
see this; and to, as well, MR & MRS D. BERLIN, Ario 15, Col. Roma
Sur, Mexico, D.F. A stranger request: I am altogether broke at the
moment & this last is my best friend, like they say, and has just got
married, and wd like him to have the little book as evidence of my joy,
etc. So, wd you be good enough to put an appropriate comment in the
front, say, 'At length the candle's out, and now, / All that they had not
done, they do./ What that is, who can tell . . .'*[7] or what you will. I'd be
grateful. You will have a taste of his sentiments in this first issue; some
things from a letter, which relate, strangely enough, to TS ELIOT. But
you will see. Anyhow, all best to you, and will write soon again, to give
you more of what's happening. You do the same.

Best,
Creeley

[*Added in pencil:*] *My wife** says: do not use this, etc. So what you
will. [*Typed:*] **She went to Black Mountain, for 2 or 3 months. I
visited. All I can remember 2 miles up a dirt road, all dressed up, lugging
a rock-like suitcase. Pretty hopeless, then. And now?

[Washington, D.C.]
tuesday [16 May 1950]

my dear RC:

    down, & off, went
    the *y & x*, to

d.b., mr & mme, with yr joy & a little epithal fr o, fr
          TROILUS, A Mask, unpublished
          [*added by Olson in margin:* ask yr
          wife to trust me, that I did all right]
& e.b., with the line, "with a nail they drew....."[8]

& the moment i can find out where [Caresse] Crosby left
more copies before she flew, the silly bird, to europe, the
silly place, you'll have replacements for yourself

got back saturday, fighting strikes and hailstones, beautiful
hailstones, killers, like baseballs, in Atlanta like grapefruit,
anyhow, like Velikovsky,[9] bolts of
nature's
reprimands:::::man has to pay, poor fly, for sticking his fingers
up her tender arse
                    i engage myself with economics also, but (4 Pages, &
          E.P.) a critique, to be serious now, must also recognize that,
          c.1917 the scientist was done as leader (econometrics included),
          c.1945, august, the political actionist likewise done

FROM THAT DATE FORWARD, man had left the only one
who, since the beginning of the species, had spent 40 hrs a day on
the problem, what is the reach of man's imagination   And the
artist knows, has known so long since deglaciation, what Miss
Benedict put thus: "that people is provided with a technique of
cultural change which is limited only by the unimaginativeness of
the human mind"[10]

              ain't that dryness true, & beauty
is difficult,
mister simpson![11]

              I suspect all clarities which lead to hate

As of education, specifically, perhaps, black mt.: you see, i only just
found out what may be the secret of why i believe in bmc; last year, i

refused to go there, to live; instead, albers[12] [*circled, with Creeley's note in margin:* a fool—but sense to know this!] had sense enough to buy my alternative: i come once a month for five days and pour out my blood

And now Robert Payne[13] tells me, that has been the base of instruction in China for 3000 yrs—the scholar lives in the imperial city, does his work, and, once a month, tells the children what he has found out

By God, that's a system. Result, one is hot. Result, kids grab. Result, you take back, blood.

As of, prose: no objection whatsoever. Only
the time has come to bust logic and para, as inherited, on the prose

> (I am, for example, delighted you have the instinct to take out passages from Berlin's letter for use in MAG—by the way, what's its name?

> Also, that you put a core in, and shoot at it.

> Also, "nothing a final block."

> Also, no long range view (this leads to world-saving).

As one particularist to another, that's what prose must be: particle by particle, clean. Prose, in contrast to verse, is a social instrument, and has shown, up to now, altogether too much of that sort of slavery: in- and de- duction. I get so sick of mags like PR, with piece after piece trying to finish themselves off, to fit an arbitrary form, never growing from the nerves of the man, always
                              —like the 4 Quartets—
                                              adjusting
themselves. And thus frauds: (I am thinking of T.S. (GI sense) Omeliot, and his use of my, *my* madonna, buono viaggi, Gloucester, and how he misuses it, is riding, is generalizer)[14]

Also, when you say, "our own way." right, right. love the Dr, love

the Master, still, even they, are in the way   There is new work
to be done, new
work

                              thanks, thanks

                              And now that i'm back
                              at my desk, maybe i'll
                              be able to get you some-
                              thing in prose as well.
                              Have one idea: a piece
                              on the secular i ripped
                              off one day a couple of
                              months ago, 5000 words in
                              one sitting, And promptly
                              forgot. [15]

                                        olson

[*Added by Creeley at top of letter:*] Olson: has THE MORNING
NEWS in the 1st issue; MOVE OVER & another in 2nd. Is doing thing
for education. The point: he comes to it: HAS got ORDER in his head,
etc. Not ALL enthusiasm. [*With arrow drawn to the following:*]Sent
to EP.

                                        [Littleton, N.H.]
                                        5/18/50

Dear Olson,
     Good to have your letter, and very good of you to have sent the

copies down to the people. Hope to be able to make this up to you, somehow, sometime. For the moment, my thanks.

These letters from you: good to have the fact of your concerns, which, as it happens, mine. The distortion that can come in with an over-emphasis or mistaking of EP's thought, or the Dr's for that matter: cripples many that wd be of use. This not to protest that I have the word from God, etc: but that I'm capable of recognizing its misuse in the hands of others: which they might take as 'friend.' Usual. But sad, as in the case of Eliot and EP.

Particulars: letters have driven me a hell of a ways from that in the past months, but also: back again. The job of making sense for a particular dozen: worse than I might take it, for the magazine, where there wont be the emphasis on 'individual' explanation, etc. I.e., some duds cant see their nose, etc. I cd name names, etc. But pointless. The point: that I find you interested and willing to help before you've seen 10 yrs of 'successful' biz.

I wd make this an offer, subject to what time you have to work with, and subject to what you may think of the 1st issue, what you can get from these letters, etc: you to judge: that if you want to take an active hand in these matters, beyond what you mean as a contributor, and as such, will count on you for staples, etc.: to take up, often, those matters pertaining to the center, by way of reviews, etc., the dirty work. Leed & I cant do it all. Some doubt now as to whether or not we can put reviews in this 1st attempt, since they are all written by the same violent hand, mine, and the rapid succession of CLIMAX, wd tell on a man. As Leed put it: this isn't criticism, it's the expression of a taste! Which, as it happens, was what I meant it to be, not taking the paraphrase, etc., the digesting of a book in public, to be the best thing you can do for it. What I wd take as better: pointing to ONE GOOD REASON why any damn fool might become less of a one, by reading it, etc. Anyhow, you will see the difficulty. Reviews, for example, cd be put to good use in this way: beyond getting to books not given general attention: that others dont treat, etc.—they can be used to cover related ground which we cant get to directly in the criticism. Just there, in other words, that anything from good housekeeping to astronomics can be made to bear: granted a head. Anyhow, that's one thing. A lot besides. Getting material: always a bug. But think it over, and we can get to the particulars when you will. You sd have a better idea than you do have before you go one way or the other, so hang on for the moment.

Prose: I cd quote you this for example from a rejection slip. 'Shows brilliance in many passages but does not have the *formality* of art. . .' That wd be Tiger's Eye.[16] It gives the game away. I.e., no one willing to risk INformal art these days, except yrs truly, and I am conducting a nation-wide search. Etc. INformal: only the 'anti-etc.' What is meant: no one willing to do more than fill forms, which they don't, god knows, even have a grip on. Take it: as it might bear: it has pained me to see the passage of the method of Dostoyevsky into the hands of Leslie Fiedler. I dont think he wd have wanted it that way. Elsewhere: the idea is to 'probe,' etc. Granted the difficulty of anyone who writes or reads poetry, and can make it: to say, seriously, that a man can be 'objective' in same: in prose, the cry. The Way. Good lord, we take one of the few rights, we do have, and toss it in the junk heap. What is 'objective': the fact that I sit here, forced to this typewriter and this paper: what I can put down: as 'subjective' as I can make it. Of course, in the popular head, imperfectly filled, now, with echoes of Rimbaud, even, they wd miss the simple sense of that 'disordering' of the senses,[17] or, later, wd miss the what the Dr. calls the necessity of destruction: that we have to tear down, destroy, even before we have any idea as to what might go up to replace, etc. (but never replace, etc.).[18] Too, the several ways in which a destruction can be put to work: in prose: a man like Stendhal wd have perfected early, an 'external' method, this to mean: a way of putting the words down, BUT wd have then set about raising hell with what thought he cd grip. Others, oddly, Joyce: held to the thinking and raised hell with the medium. Odd, that the smoothest way cd house the chaos, as with Stendhal, etc. That cd take him to: 'As an honourable man who abhors exaggeration, I do not know what to do. . .'[19] I wd not mistake the external ordering of a way: either in prose or in poetry, as the only seat for 'change.' It can happen in the head in other ways & be there to be seen. For some: almost an impossible impediment to HAVE to PUT it in WORDS. But, for this time: guts gone out of prose altogether, and I am no less guilty than others, and have to put more of what's here, into there. I had thought: it's time for who's talking to be more than a voice, monotone, etc. It had been that way; time to get back on the track, granted none has ever existed, and that no mean problem. Anyhow, in Unamuno: there is a fight between who's writing and who's being written. Now it gets to a battle between not only those, for that was subject against who was making him: but a battle against the whole process of words, the compulsion, to make CLEAR again, why in hell we keep at it. What stake a reader might have in that: I wdn't know: but expect, he'd call it, interesting. Take it: the fight will come to 'why do I write today . . . '[20] & until we get better answers that [i.e. than] PR & Co. can put out, and they have some lulus (which I had the benefit of getting straight from the horse's ass, [Delmore] Schwartz) — things will be quiet.

No one ever picked up on D.'s Notes From Underground; no one ever picked up on any of S. [Added: these 2 wd be the basis for a compre- hension of pssble ways in prose.] It's still there. What the head cd get to: what the head cd get to. I.e., elsewhere I see 'list of plots' advertised. Not even funny. That it sd be dark, and 100 miles from coherence, or any of the pleasantries: and someone suggests: I haven't a point of my own.

Of course, there are damn few that cd bring even in Lawrence's strength to it, granted that man's 'unpopularity' at the moment & granted Miller is 2/3 sheer fudge. The only horror text I can think of outside of Kafka: and that is damned imperfect: Valery. And I shiver reading that much more than I do when reading K. And too: some of Stevens. 'What will they think of — next . . . '

Write when you can—   Best—
Creeley

Note: enclose letter from the old man.[21] He asks for samples of my printing-partners. Sent him a letter from Leed/ from B. Berlin/ & this one today from you. I.e., the half/assed stuff he sent me: needed some antidote. And hope I have not misrepresented yr thoughts, etc. I *do* think: you put the matter there: straight. And to prove I didnt leave you hanging, etc., will enclose section from letter I answered the enclosed with—put in with yrs & the rest.

Olson— —
Part of the letter: [*added by Olson:* (to Pound, in answer to, PROGRAM, & [sent on? slur on?] olson)]

Abt programs, etc.: wd take yr notes as basic, etc. BUT wd not have my own attitude confused with the alternative— 2. The point: what good is a declaration of policy: if that policy is no more than the declaration, etc. Given: a 'policy' is what wd determine the selection of material: if no material can be taken as an instance of the policy other than in a most oblique way: of what USE is the policy, etc., but to prove us duds and sloganeers. I have noted the difficulty (extreme) of finding material to concur with the limited program you suggest: that difficulty is still the same, and I see no immediate chance of its getting 'solved,' etc. Ringer: [22] has not written in reply to my letter, the one which he notes in his own. Horton: has yet to do more than echo, and advise, etc. And wd take you as filling the bill on this last, and since he has nothing MORE to offer—of what use? Paquette: wd count on him for occasional poems, but I cant see that he has the head for what the job is: the job, at least, to make concrete what 4PP, et alia, 'suggest.' Things like the Cleaners Manifesto, [23] granted the validity of pt. 3—pt 1 still hopeless: '. . . what is really going on . . . .' To mean: I have no use for that method. Put up—OR shut up. 4PP hopelessly limited by space, but since we will have the room—useless not to make use of it. Take it this way:

1. We resent the falsification of history.
   We resent the misrepresentation of thought.
   We resent the misuse of ideas.

2. We do not want any contributors who do not resent it.
   We do not want any contributors who do not resent it.
   We do not want any contributors who do not resent it.

I.e., it can certainly be said: better.

Witness: the nature of the 3 precepts put down in 1912 re Imagism. I.e., exact, pointed, no fuzz, applicable. I take it: what a program should hit: NOT somebody else's 'method' (*the falsification of history*: real: but that which must be got to by way of a counter-method); not a prescription that those not sympathizing will not be tolerated (this wd follow like the night the day, etc.): BUT a statement of direction, of concern (BEYOND resentment), of method; which can attack, by its own nature, this falsification; and which can get beyond it to something to [be] made USE of, directly. There, the issue abt those not wanted, abt toleration, non-resentment, risk, & the like: wd be something to take seriously. Not 'I dont like newspapers' but 'this is exactly what I think they should be.' It brings things out in the open: demands clarity from us & from any possible readers. As yr program wd stand: it wd allow any idiot, with any idiotic, half-assed 'resentment' to take complete advantage of our 'resentment': to be buddies, etc. What this wd give the opposition, say: I shudder to think. In any event: I wd take it: a program must be clear enough to commit its backers to 'specifics,' to avoid generalities, to avoid misunderstanding. I cd not see making it less, etc., etc., etc.

"This sounds too much like Dan'l Webster for my complete mental comfort but, generally speaking, that is where I stand." [*Added in margin:* the Dr.][24]

Yr lad—
C.

[Littleton, N.H.]
Monday
[22 May 1950]

Dear Olson,

Word has it that you have written a book on Melville. Is this true.

What else might I get my hands on, that you have put down in the way of poetry.

What is the TROILIUS (?)? Beyond being unpublished.

Notes from P—35 yr interim—still make this; from de Gourmont, as P put it/ almost the whole 'law & gospel'; then, it was ALSO a letter.

'd'écrire franchement ce qu'il pense—seul plaisir d'un écri-vain. . . '25

That same source: '. . . a satire upon stupidity, an attack. It is the weapon of intelligence at bay; of intelligence fighting through an alignment of odds. . . ' 1915.

Will trust you for some of this. Write when you can.

All best to you,

Creeley

For the first: the initial confusion coming from a vague reference to Chas Olson, Sr. & 'the other.' What is that. I.e., if you HAVE written a bk on Melville, I expect it wd be, like they say, 'inneresting.' As you will.

hate to not be able to give you 'good news' with every letter abt our 'progress.' Inescapable that a certain amt will be backwards, at the beginning. I.e., we take it of absolute importance that we have a grip, exact, on what we take it we're up to, what we 'want,' more than to say: geewhiz, good stuff, etc. So I have to keep thrashing it out with my boy Leed, printer & fellow Jesus, etc. I.e., to get rid of the hodgepodge, and tighten er up into something sharp. He still wants: broadsides: i.e., that a printing of one man's work, at random intervals, i.e., 'think ten poems of Olson, eg, in one broadside lump, would have more force than this hodgepodge . . . ' Well, dammit, he misses this fact: that if you can indicate, put down, a precise, a grip, an attack on what's rotten to let such cases as yrself go their way, FREE of shit & impedimenta: the greatest. I.e., a magazine will have the advantage: of making explicit, what one wd take to be the key of yr own salvation, etc. Of using divers such salvations as the basis for an 'understanding' of aht, etc. Also: he doesn't grip how damn often, and how usual, one man's work in the format he intends, can go right to the bottom, without one noticing same. But he *is* right: in saying that more grip, tighter context, must be got. As soon as I can say, exactly, what you cd do to help: will most certainly, let you know.

C.

this might, now, be to the point: some note from you as to what you yrself wd like to hit on the education, and when you might be able to get to same.

Emerson hitting 'poet as pedant': am still waiting to see it. But keep to the style, etc., you name in yr last letter. It has to be that way.

[Washington, D.C.]
wednesday   may 24   L

my dear creeley:

i suppose, normally, on the assumption that you are already possessed of enough olson, i'd be shipping this[26] off to some one of those sheets which you and i have our opinion of

and i dare say that is what shall be done (for some reason i have magner of glass hill[27] in the back of my bean)

but, because you are you, i want you (and leeds, if you will) to have a look at it now that it is done, for what pleasure and use it may give you this is first copy, and, on the assumption you are loaded now, and you'll have first pick on anything else that comes up in the future, will you ship this back to me when you have had sufficient chance to digest same?   then i'll run it on to magner—or, if you should have any other notion of live, semi-life MAG, i should be grateful for it

((which reminds me: do you [know] kitasono, of VOU? the feller who wrote "The Shadow"?[28] he has been publishing me in japan, and i should like you two to be put together, if you are not, already   I had a letter this week from another magazine there, asking, at Kitasono's suggestion, that I do piece on verse in amurrika. but that's not conceivable—i don't know it—but i think i will shoot them over the PRO-verse thing   I bring it up because it suggests that VOU may have folded ((I haven't heard from K since he published "Preface," and I sent him "The Kingfishers" (you will have that shortly, in the 1st no. of the Montevallo Review)   The new magazine's name is, SHIGAKU, a monthly, they say, in their canny-uncanny english, "the *only* and the most influential monthly magazine on poetry, with a circulation of 7000 copies," the editor Isaku Hirai

((it was my impression that the greeks and the japanese were carrying forward Ez and Bill's work (eliot, too, in case i'm not interested in, seferis)   But poulos,[29] just here fr greece, says the push (it was partisan, strong) has been badly broken by the reaction: most of the poets and painters are rotting in the Cyclades camps, or being destroyed by such punishments as, to put them and two cats in a potato sack tied at the waist, and then to drop the man & his into a barrel of water.

So kitasono, and his fellows?

okay

o

[*signed:*] olson

[Washington, D.C.]
(later, wed., may 24 L)

sez i, on the phone, to my wife, to whom, i suppose
it is, substantially, written, "it's an

    antey-dantey"

and, once out of my mouth, sez i, to her, i wish
i'd sd that to creeley!

        So i do.

          o
    [signed:] Olson

---

*[The opening sections of the following, up to "In yr letters . . . ," were
crossed out by Olson. See his June 8 letter to come and his occasional
marginal comments noted throughout below.]*

[Littleton, N.H.]
Wednesday
[24 May 1950]

Dear Olson,
    Well—you push, and good that you do. Yesterday, had been busy
with the work here: cleaning, up, and very remote: a lot that should be
right in the hand.
    Some notes on the thing abt the projective verse vs.
non-projective. *[Added by Creeley in margin: All this: a tangent.
Followed by: will get to it again.]* The musical phrase: that wd point to

the 'voice' or what constitutes, better, more exact: what is to be heard (this to be taken as 'analogy'). Two things we have yet to pick up on—with the head: a feel for TIMING, a feel for SOUND . . . & when, at those times of practice, you hit: these were an overt part of it: yes, that was in it. Not much to go on, now: other than Williams, or EP. THO: a listening to Gertrude Stein will demonstrate a damn clear grip on just this thing you are writing abt. An analogy: viz current 'hatred' of this man: Charlie Parker: even among his own group: and to be put with him, Max Roach, Miles Davis, Bud Powell, et alia: the point: here, TOO, a hatred for that which breaks out, or extends the FORM, the only FORM:— what IS there, in any given instance. Granted: we cannot take over exactly: this example, of what timing, variation, & a sound-sense can COMPLETE: it is worth the time & trouble to listen, since it in the case of Bird, etc.: is a precise example of the consciousness necessary, in a basic form: or character. Difficult to figure precisely, for one's own use, or anyone's: how much the 'intentional' broadening of 'getting to people' with a 'good' poem: FORMALIZED, CONCRETIZED: this way out. Parallel instances: a universal language: formalization, to make 'simple,' etc: difficult to say what this might have been responsible for: in this hardening of the arteries. Or putting aside: of major components. BECAUSE it is precisely that which you note: which makes the welding, fusing: of any poem: and damn those who say different. WHAT ELSE? :

that the emphasis is now on 'speech' patterns: demonstrates: how difficult it is to get back to the able distortion of the Gks. Like Miles Davis' group being delighted with the SOUND of a French horn. And leaving it to his own wind: to make the NECESSARY: dissonance.

Anyhow, I read this with a good deal of respect: etc. (because I'm damned if I'll put the lid on anything like that, ETC.).

The other thing: too much. Will send it on to Leed: and will at least give him the chance to see what can be done. Cannot now say when it could be used. [*Added by Creeley in margin:* viz. note later] I.e., am not sure that the job is not: in one aspect: a systematic disorganization, etc. Familiar enough. But he is headed on the education: and think for our own coherence: may be best to aim at that directly for the first two or three: as planned: but something like this cd go, as well. A little time: will write abt it soon: but this is the best thing yet. I.e., today came from D[orothy] P[ound] as well: the Hudson Review on these same things: but useless to comment: that aside from what EP has there: not much of the man. [*Added by Creeley:* well—the long thing on the Cantos, I dunno.][30] And have from yr own thing: the first full grip on him: I've yet had. Had used the Dr's piece in The Doc No. of the Briarcliff Quarterly for a perspective these past 4 months: the letter to an australian editor: too much.[31] But it has to be that WAY.

[*Added by Olson in margin:* date of this *May* 12-14? (pulled out 4 pages, 2 double, & send [*sic*] to Creeley 6/8/50, to return)]

In yr letters: abt EP and the program: that is something that I had figured, and when Leed wrote: a program like EP HAD: cd not see it: or cd see that that might be the program I wanted, since it never was, etc. The point here: had taken it: EP moved from one thing to another, with the eyes opened: and how much is the result of having been in A with B waiting for C: useless to conjecture. But it was: what was: at hand, in the hand. Always: and nothing anywhere: to indicate a long-range view like they say: but the repetition of the key phrase: from de Gourmont: which is 'interesting' & the emphasis on NON-conclusion that the Kung or Lao-Tsze (?) wd get to: since given the process: there is no end: etc.
                              BUT a way of dealing with everything that might come to hand: all the work: proves that.

Well, let this go for now. Will get to this soon again. And will let you know what is happening. Am very glad that these things come. That you are there, in brief. Hope that some time: wd cd meet, etc., or talk, or get to these things in person. Must count on the letters for now. Wd wonder: do you make NY now and again: let me know when you might be there: allow myself one visit or so: a year: to talk to one or two: and no point in NOT making it coincide with yr own plans. So much for that.

                    Best to you,
                        Creeley

Why not make it up here: whenever possible: a good place to sit down.

What my boy Leed calls: revision of thought.

Interesting, like they say, in MAKE IT NEW: the placement of the thing on James after the thing on de Gourmont: 2 sides of the same penny . . .[32] A point. /I.e., I see, later, looking again, the point: on the piece on EP, IS NOT to, say, print it, (1), but to read it (1), and to see what you stand as: etc. Well, that wd be it anyhow. And, if nothing comes of the gig with the Dr., perhaps we cd get to this, when you will. Reading such stuff: granted one is up to what I am: you get grabby, etc. Anyhow, let that sit for the moment.

    See, too, you did write the bk on Melville. What is this abt. What wd you hit there (1).

    Wish that I cd document my own stand with this clarity. (Nostalgia). But at this point: these things come to method: granted the push to that, by way of the root.

    Who writes/ and why, etc. What is up. "Love God," Pico writes to Angelo Polit[i]an, "we rather may, than either know Him, or by speech utter Him. And yet had men liefer by knowledge never find that which they seek, than by love possess that thing, which also without love were in vain found . . ." [*Added by Creeley in margin:* beautiful thing—sound—Malory—o' course.] The heresy, being that last line: or what wd now pass for same. Bitter to 'expand' such a thing—by comment. From Pater, who says later: 'It remained for a later age to conceive of effecting a scientific reconciliation of Christian sentiment with the imagery, the legends, the theories about the world, of pagan poetry and philosophy. For that age the only possible reconciliation was an imaginative one . . .'[33] [*Added by Creeley:* what a *Shit*—]

[*Note by Olson in margin:* Start here: *with another note by Olson at top of page:* RETURN TO OLSON (despite the law!)]

No. no such clarity. Rather: the oblique: afraid of conclusions:

sounds: and the oddness. Can remember, very well, the meeting with
Slater Brown: who had been B. in the Enormous Room[34] (and almost
like a fairy-tale) you wd remember that he had been there: abt a good
time: before C arrived: and looking there again: you wd see that B, not
C, was the touchstone. Now: a bitter & pathetic man: but had been
with him, long enough to see what it might be like: NOT to be Ezra: or
to have been one of the pathetic group: circa 1925—who wd have been
in London, assembled for the 'expatriate' issue of Transition: by
Malcolm C[owley], and what a windbag he is, ho ho
(altho—caution—some gd things he did—too) and the rented rooms &
typewriters & wine: all there, by Malcolm's hand 'thinking' that NO
ONE wd think of imbibing before he had writ his mite: for the cause.
He still hangs to that gay way: or so I wd take it. But B. He makes me
remember another man, not got to, even, mostly, forgotten: you wd
remember? Hart Crane. And what ever happened to him, beyond 'Hey
Hart, Dont Jump,' and NO etc. But B. One night was with him in an
old studio: a series: of same: & Peter Neagoe [*added by Creeley:*
nearby—an old fool—like.]: identified as the recipient of 'I cant bloody
well be bothered to write my OWN biography . . .' (a death mask):
and people had been there: we were being paid for by two middle-aged
women: & can remember on the 3rd (?) day: meaning to go to the
bathroom: and falling down a whole flight of stairs, to hit the door at
the bottom, & out: into bright sunlight: on the lawn. & there: B's wife
& little girl: looking for father. Anyhow, the night in question:
everyone gone: a big storm comes up: off the water as they will: and
the whole place shaking: thunder: rain like drums: flashes of bright
light: and then: B starts chanting: [*note by Olson in margin:* all above,
just for THIS] LO LORD THOU RIDEST, LORD LORD THY
SWIFTING HEART NOT STAYETH NOR NOW BIDETH BUT
SMITHEREENED APART, etc.[35] I misquote, etc. [*Added by Olson in
margin:* THEN THIS, *with line enclosing rest of letter.*] No, no direct
way to anything. Never back, say. Here: wife & little boy: she has
$185 per month & that plus chickens & the small farm carry us.

I had
wanted to strip, make clean, all that wd leak in by way of an excess of
goodwill, even of love. Well: this is no living for a man who likes sun,
etc. And a climate: where head is head, etc., and no shit. Cold: 60
below for 3 months, say, and to go out: bite. Cannot put up with what

doesn't bear, because it is too cold. To bother.

Sometimes I don't believe, or think, it will be possible to go anywhere. That when I was younger, and I couldn't be much younger than at the (this) moment: well, then to travel: and we had planned to live in Switzerland, in Mexico: you name it. No work for these hands. But their own.

A yng man: wd do well to consider what or wherein: wd best appear: the marks of his age. Phew: says the Doc. & right.

No, no old men: cannot make their way, their morals, or their sense: but wherein: love wd revive: antient person of my heart. Said one. Yes.

You are right: 'but for clarity on where you and your fellow citizens ARE': they'll get you for that. And will hope to be catching them: myself. Clarity, dammit, & a way of making CLEAR: what in essence is.

Yr. boy,
Creeley

Etc

Sd have noted something abt Paul Goodman: both from yr hitting of him, and what my own slant might be. I had argued for the novels, elsewhere, letters, & talk. That they were good, and were more than I'd found around in the way of other men's efforts. The criticism: a headache. Have not enough familiarity with it to make a comment, but for the place here: it seemed now & again, as with the Father Of The Psychoanalytic Movement,[36] that there was something to look at.

Take it: wd have respect, certainly, for that which capable of shaking up the static contexts into which a thought, idea, or manifestations of same: had been holed. At times: (many times in the novels) PG is capable, by my own thought, of making this. I do not sympathize or have much grip on the motives: or what I would take as: both the raison d'être or the raison d'écrire—etc. Useless to point to, perhaps, the utter uselessness : of amalgamating a private, and rightly so, slant: for purposes of a 'general' comment. I had met him abt a year ago: he

is a good friend of Leed's & an odd mixture these two: Leed, abt 5'9":
26 yrs, heavy, boned face: tho not 'sad' but, otherwise: living, the
whole of it: and somewhat ape-like in placing of arms, etc: power in
chest, etc. And hair going back, receding: making long temples. And
Goodman: somewhat the cast of a wizened, delighted old man:
monkey like: the mouth, & slight lisp, blond, but more yellow: hair;
also small, tho lighter than Leed: and that felt difference between
them, which wd come to yr thing: 'Womman is mannes joye and al his
blis . . .'[37] To be for Leed: while for PG: it is the cast, always, of an
intricate complexity: out of which he gets out: by wit. But Leed like
any of those heavy-coated, short dogs in summer: panting, and not
giving much away. As he said: 'Full of phlegm & built to endure . . .'
Abt it: and for PG: hard to say what that one time cd tell of him, or of
the reading: one gets at the delight, easy, a great lightness to him & his
words. Leed: moves much lower & deeper, and my own ways are that
way: so feel closer, certainly, to him. L'enfant terrible . . . wd be abt
it. Taking who has been called that; and who will be, etc., into
acct.

I dont know: mostly since Leed has sent PG's things this
way; with that friendship between them: taken as leaven. It made
them better. Bud Berlin: hates the man but likes the writing, and
expect, if I do much one way or the other: wd get to that myself. He is
a charlatan of an intricate sort. And a head, too, not to be forgotten. I
wd say: such a head: wd delight in the kind of occasion that Freud wd
be: be for. Otherwise: much that is of use I wd take it: in the novels. I
had the liking a year ago, when Leed sent them. Expect that I wd still
have, tho impossible to date these impressions, that same thing.

There are, as it turns out, abt 4–5 who come close enough to one's own
way, to get strength from it: and vice versa. Elsewhere: all the 'related'
material. PG wd fall into that last. And all the shit: to be
forgotten.

PG is still a kid, or wd want you to think so. The curse
of that: that it maintains that boyishness, etc. With PG, and the wife &
kid: impossible to say what a quiet meal with them: was.

at bay? and who isn't, *what* force of man isn't—even those who are
not quite intelligent and not wholly stupid?

agreed, the weapon *is* the real one, agree, it must, *forever*, fight, stay
cornered, like a Texan keep its shoes on and
its back to a wall

agree its dance, among syllables,[38] is
the ultimate necessity

yet, 35 yrs out, we are not, no longer are we
REFORMERS, we
are too dry
for dreams, we
are not as hard as youth, we
are as hard as
anything can be made to be

> ((h melville wrote for the whole of his
> later life with, over his desk, this:
> "keep true to the dreams
> of thy youth"[39]

> bah, him, bah
> Ez: each,
> to his time))

which goes for us, too, i mean the time,
not
the dream

Is it not rather handsome, and gain, that we have lowered
the sights?

                    (I imagine one omeros, and, say, to go into the camp of
                    the tribe of Ezra, one dante, also felt
                    that the task was, satire on
                    surrounding stupidity)

What we take as—I think we can quietly say, with no arrogation—
both more simply and more tragically (to dare to use a pumped out word)
what the Fox sd to Possum one good day: "It ain't original sin that
did us in, it war o-riginal, in-nate, stoo-pidity!"[40]

And ain't that true.

So what do we do? fall for the corporate state? save the Constitution?
use niggers and jews as x's—"here is mud, here is
                              usura"

                              AND THEN, when we are 58, find out
who gives boxes marked xxx, where
tristesse
can be written on?

The GLORY of the o.m. is: that he learned
FROM OUR TIME!

                         And for this we forgave him,
                         and, as we walked on,
                         over our shoulders, we tipped
                         our hands

For OUR JOB is,
(did I say?)
now that he got the fat out,
our job is,
to get rid of
his sneer:

man is larger than

his social reformation

This, it seems to me, is where our fathers all date, give us
stale bread
(tho god save us—Ezra will if He won't!—from all
fatuity!

))))))))))(((((((((

troilus, i'm afraid, except for, perhaps, such lines as went to berlin,
came acropper

the verse is scatt'red (i'll keep it
comin at you as
it comes to hand)—i think there is
one you might fancy, in WESTERN R,
Spring, 1947, "There Was A Youth
Whose Name Was Thomas Granger"

the melville book was CALL ME ISHMAEL,
reynal, now harcourt, 1947
and do keep talkin to me
the problemes: i'm
heatin up

yrs, in the midst of another poem of love to
the same, which, i'm afraid is, what is the severest
problem,
the lyric mode[41]

(Miss Sappho, be
my potenta![42]   Olson

[Littleton, N.H.]
5/26/50

Dear Olson,

The poem today: too much. That line, word: like a pile driver, or what they say: Man, you are breaking it up, you are in yr crib. Real groovy. Anyhow, very good: take it, as it comes at you: no TIME to duck, and that is too much: a BIG question.

Will make a copy to send on to Leed, and for myself. And will get this back to you, shortly. Will try to keep the hands clean, etc. Once we get set: wont have to turn these things away; and it hurts.

Magner: hard to take seriously, a man who is capable of such looseness, etc. I.e., everything there, like they say. And look in vain for more than one or two: to have grip, etc. Even the few that do: are lost in the wash. His program: now that IS something. [*Added:* Phew—as the doc says.] Wd think much better: to send this on to Dick Emerson: GOLDEN GOOSE: I had copied out for him the one abt NE: MOVE OVER——you shits. &: Green is the color of my true love's green/ despite/ New England is/ despite her merchants & her morals, etc., etc. No, the end. That last four line bit: being one of the nicest 'handlings' of sequence, etc: have yet seen. You got it, old sport. Anyhow, Emerson: had asked abt where to get a copy of Y&X: had written him abt it: has not sd whether or not he got it: also has not written abt the poem: but noted in his last: that he wd get to it, and sounded pleasant. He is apt to give some space, I think: in a good way; and does not, like Magner, make it an ashcan. Emerson's address: 1927 Northwest Blvd., Columbus 12, Ohio. Tell him Joe sent you.

Otherwise, it is hard to figure wherelse. Emerson has the same concerns/ has himself a good grip/ good firm line & language. I wd try him. I know very damn little abt what is up with the little mags, and have taken that on as one part of the current effort. Knew nothing six months ago/ beyond what was in the bkshops: the usual. And that didn't seem it. Will note here one on [*i.e.* of] my own headaches: and/or, where to send prose (stories), not that I wd put too much weight on them, tho a few: yes, dammit. But have gone the rounds without much luck/ tho did crack, oddly, KENYON with one for this summer issue: (the worst & wdn't yez know it . . .).[43] Anyhow, I'm the boy who just picked up 1 er 2 at the local bkshoppe, and let er rip: and now, sadly, FIND that I am supposed to keep tabs on their taste: as well as my own. So anyone you might be able to point to: re prose: wd be a help.

See you will appear in IMAGI: and that is good. Hard of me not to get grabby, but will most certainly hope you get in everywhere you can: for, is it not true: that IS the point.

Kitasono: had seen the things in the Quarterly Review (& there is one 1st class idiot: WEISS)-nicht)[44] Anyhow: had seen that; and the note abt the group: tho this puzzled: 'Directed originally by the thinking of T. E. Hulme, the group since the war has extended his ideas into Dadaism . . . (?????). Probably, the idiot at it: again. Anyhow, should like very much to make what can be made: with Kitasono. Say what to do, etc.

While yr at it: make a random list: of any magazines you can think of, here or elsewhere: that it wd be good to pick up on. Ones, preferably, with heads. When you will.

Best to you,
Creeley

[*Added at top of letter:*] If Emerson cant use this, or if he cant give you a very good damn reason for not using this: he's not the one I take him for. He sd: pick up.

EP continues to nail em: on the nose/ with the method. A great help.

[*On small slip of paper enclosed, referring to "In Cold Hell":*]
Crazy stuff. My only kick: (beginning) section: 'Language, etc.' & in 4 (1st half) 'And shall you blame those, etc,' to go to: 'Yes . . . (being too much, from there on in . . .). Anyhow, one man's opinion/ and it cd certainly carry it/ all/ as it stands.

sat/ 5-27-50/ wash

cree-
ley:
tanks,
tanks

    especially wish i had sd (you will, you will!)[45]

> "Two things we have yet to pick up on—with the head:
> a feel for TIMING, for
> SOUND
>
> & when you hit,
> these are an overt part, they
> were in it"

    say, why don't i slug that in, in copy? any objections? introduced
thus: "Creeley's gloss, here, is helpful: . . ." ?

    and the 1st page sure needs some such hard-headedness: i never
did get back enuf enthusiasm to double-hammer it

    also like yr equivalence of consciousness & character in:

> "is a precise example of the consciousness necessary,
> in a basic form: or character"

(if i am right to take

you as meaning character in what was an old sense)

    & the area, when does the INformal become FORmal: did a
wire recording of IN COLD HELL the other night, for experiment,
with friend r[udd] fleming, and his 1st response was, this is not
"available" enuf for "projective." But then, 2nd reading, he
wondered. I don't. The thing is, to go on, BY BREATH, hammering
out the INform. & keep at it. It's going to be somebody else's business
to say, see, hear, eventually, what's been done. I distrust these poetic

dramatists.

It is here again c. 1825 Bolyai Farkas, to Bolyai Janos: "Son, when men are needed they spring up, on all sides, like violets, come the season."[46] One says, one's own ear. And works. Let the audience spring up. (Which, in no sense, of course, is Joyce: I expect my audience to devote their lives, to my work.[47] Here, sneer, alsowieder.[48])

Tell me, Creeley, do you not, yourself, make with verse? If not, it is clearly, from this letter (passages on yrself, & on S. Brown), the answer to yr questions abt. prose. And *method.*

Also agree, "the job: systematic disorganization": which goes for a MAG and for a MAP and for MAK-a-pome: composition in field is such.

& yr ps on PG is okay with me. As a matter of fact I have like affections, and less than the necessary respects. All I was teeing off on, was Pound's joining of good-man &
old-son.
I took it, it was loaded. The old bastard has pulled an inversion of himself to peg me: told Lekakis i was
Semite & World-Saver,
recently. The "Semite" was fr a trap I layed (for DP as well as hE) abt my Swdish ancestry (very factual; that the family name Lybeck was Lubeck, was, sd my Grandmother, Hungarian; but so put the moving of people across Europe led HE.P and Damn.P to think.....
a trap on purpose laid to make the taker mad[49]

& World-Saver? jee-zus, i leave such to pounds, and goodmans!

This is just a note to get back to you the enclosed corre-

spondence fr He-Whom-the-Doc-Calls-Part Womrat-Part
SKUNK:

please keep me in touch with any further swipes. (What you
have done is let off the steam, both over there across the river,[50] and
over here, by the railroad tracks. And it is very healthy for all the
young concerned, who shuttle back and forth. You will know, of
course, that I shall, because I do not believe that any meannesses
should be added to this great man, keep what you let me know to
home. I value it, for fix, on myself. For he is one /true / immediate /
predecessor.)

Suggestion: if you should care to pluck one other thing from 4
Ps, I call to yr attention the poem which seems to me still the single fine
poem the Old Men thereafter, Kitasono's A SHADOW, in issue #6,
June '48. (I could try, if you are interested, to get a true copy from K: the
punctuation is miserably garbled in it as is.)

Write, as you so accurately say,
when you can

Olson

[*Added in ink:*]
p.s.

in enclosing, have just reread P's : nothing,
nothing in it but, what I sent you on penny pc!
just nothin'
am amazed

Never thot I'd live to see etc
"EP 35 yrs behind
the time"![51]

PSS
What does the tag "too much" you use, mean?

[Littleton, N.H.]
Sat/
[27 May 1950]

Dear O,

and why not a little sugar/ by way of an opening/ and why not: 'Poems by Olson were. . . too much. . . Cannot believe him, it is so rare that he is all one might say . . . For he does write so very great . . .' From E. Baron/[52] so not in vain. Etc.

Other things: today along with yr own/ a letter from Gordon Ringer/ who I think may be a boy for the education whirl// has the head & the motives & the facts. Willing: and hope he can put it down. Useless to say: what: until I see what he turns in. Also today the letters, etc. back from EP: (and had included yr own THE MORNING NEWS & MOVE OVER [*added:* also letter noted elsewhere] to show him what I took to be of use, etc.) with this note by his right hand/DP: 'E.P. much too exhausted to advise on ms/ and in any case has been long convinced that no one can usefully do this for the generations that come after him . . .' Ho Ho. And what have you been up to/ old sport/ and what was that abt: 'fatuity . . .'??? What is this wife like, he has? Who takes that tone with ME, DAMMIT??? O well: a joke. And put against that constant hand/holding of the past 3 months/ a good joke. At least she quotes him on Leed: 'He finds your printer "simpatico."'

Of course: time comes to push off from that particular shore. For whatever.

The only possible 'reforming' cd be done in 2 ways: what EP had called that category of criticism which meant: in new composition, which I wd lump with his 'criticism by practice of style in a given period,' etc., & the biz abt translation.[53] And there is that reforming which takes upon itself: the clearing of ground to make room/ for what 'might' be of value/ etc. In each case: it wd be better not to take on the usual face of a reformer: granted the means toward such 'reformation' in each case: have an end of their own/ or sd have. Well, that is old stuff. But it isn't 'reformers,' etc. Make new: is the kick.

Speaking of HM/ as I was abt 5 hrs ago now/ and your mention of the thing over the desk, etc. Wd you know this of Blake's (not only by way of swapping grrreat wurds, etc.): 'Thou art a Man, God is no more/ Thine own humanity learn to adore . . .'[54] which Bud Berlin had written me of, saying that Gide quotes that in the Journals (which I remember, etc.) but then adds: that he did not go on/ as Blake did to: 'This drawing was done above Thirty Years ago, and proves to the Author, and he thinks to any discerning eye, that the productions of our youth and of our maturer age are equal in all essential points . . .' Dont ask me why, etc., just that it went deep/ if only into Blake. Anyhow, abt the bistros, etc., there was this word: *to each his natural own.* It goes.

If I cd only keep at IT: or bear on this one thing, under hand, but my head runs. At the moment: to Stevens: '.............
>   A.   A violent order is disorder; and
>   B.   A great disorder is an order. These
>   Two things are one. (Pages of illustrations)....'[55]

But home again, etc.

Other things: had whacked at Leed this morning abt the biz of the new romanticists, etc., Rule Britannia, etc. I.e., cannot think that they are the ones/ to bring guts back to the wasteland, etc. Cannot think/ that anything 'but great clarity can cut thru . . . .'[56] Do not think they have it. To be sure, now & again/ something to admire & wd that good intentions & a love: cd build more than claptrap. To hell with that. Wd make use of what was of use: there/ anywhere: but wd not 'subscribe' to that out. To hit them: as the 'noo' saviours: is to forget that a constant opp/ has been up against Auden & co/ etc. For many yrs. If only these: the dr, stevens, moore, ep, etc. THEY carried the weight/ and useless to shift it/ at this late date/ to a bunch of sun/daft daisy pickers. What people miss: that one Dylan Thomas can carry you a long way from HOME: and the night comes on: fast. Have never quite made/ why more didnt pick up on his prose/ and let the poetry/ stand as good/ but no end. And will you tell me why: Edith Sitwell: is

taken to be 'significant.' With the exception of abt 6 poems: I dont &
cant make that stuff. [*Last four sentences enclosed in brackets, "Dylan
Thomas" underlined with the following added in margin:* But a
different point here/ than with the romanticists, etc./ more like Kafka.]

Then there seems to be a whole body of prose/ which for one catch or
another/ is never made use of. Useless to define it here/ any man wd
have a right to call it what he thought, etc. Just so long as it was
gripped: that much of use had been kicked out. Not only *the wan-
derer*/[57] etc., but so much that I wd take to be around/ and cant find/
like w. lewis, etc./ what must be in italy & france/ but just doesn't get
thru. Real fog.

Had looked to Durrell for some good stuff/ and now wonder what's
happened to him. Had looked to the same from Berryman/ after the
long home, etc./ narcissus/ etc.[58] And then hit that inane thing abt EP
in poetry/ that is pathetic.

It was when I said,
"There is no such thing as truth,"
That the grapes seemed fatter.
The fox ran out of his hole . . .

Shit [*with arrow drawn back to "abt EP in poetry . . ."*].

Yes, a good deal of that.

Yr note abt: man is larger than his social reformation/ the thing. The
point missed by them: that given the 'reformation'/ there was supposed
to be some one: THERE. O well/ clear enough. & you are right.

antedante/ yes: good to find someone who's coming thru, etc.

well/ Goodbye, Mrs. Pappadopoulos, and thanks/[59]
to them/

for yourself/ all best & will write soon again.

Creeley

Have written Emerson abt the chance he might be getting the long poem/ not to stack the deck/ tho, yes, if it can be/ but am interested to get his comment on yr work. Forgive me for making it the password/ but I lack a better one at the moment. (this soup: but you can make the point, etc.)

[Littleton, N.H.
ca. 28 May 1950]
strictly ANON/ commun/

Along The Atonal Trail

Re the prose/ and what might be up here & there with that. And re the effort, generally, to get to energies/ and to make the magazine/ review/ or what you will/ more than dead tripe. Had figured that the sickness in prose/ was a great deal worse, say, or less noted/ than that with poetry. Have wondered now & again, why EP had put the weight on James/ and beyond the fact of the contemporary biz, he wuz around, it wd probably be: that poetry was doing prose's work in those days/ even with Joyce. No one has put the finger on, precisely, what the difference is between what's up/ in either. Or Ez had it: prose is primarily an indictment of an intolerable condition/ or at least/ negative in the sense it is apt to come out of a strong dislike/ rather than, shall we say, joy/ etc.[60] Valery had it: likewise. Of course: Lewis, and Joyce, and Stendhal/ but Ez was not looking for the main thing in prose: or reach, centered in ONE intelligence/ which can dominate, by grip & a weird sort of vicarious living, an ENTIRE area right down to the little weeds in the garden. I wd take it: the insistence on methodology/ together with the emphasis on 'values' & manner/ wd put him on to Stendhal/ in a way/ NOT what S. might have wanted// was looking for kicks even/

like a man wd want to hear one great chord/ again & again. Have
wondered, perhaps, why there was never the bearing on Melville or
Dostoyevsky or the ½ dozen others that have done things in prose &
to it. Remember in the case of Lawrence: and of course: WHAT that
kind of relation cd NOT be, etc., or where Lawrence refers to the
Pound person who is bothering him for a contribution to one of the
'anthologies,' etc. (Good lord, who IS alone, like a novelist???). Well,
looking for 'ways' in prose. I have never been able to make much with
H. James: had read a bit, younger, & cold, fish-like stuff: it is. It's the
head that cd make it/ but dry stuff for the blood, etc. And, no, dammit,
it is not important. (Or 'history,' perhaps, yes, it cd go there, and be
brought in there: record: but a novelist??? Shit: he's been cut half
dozen ways . . .)   Anyhow, a young man looking back over those
green yrs: wd have to throw out one hell of a lot: Forster, Barnes, one
hell of a lot of Joyce, Proust, go very damn slow with Kafka, (Lewis??
jesus: what is wrong there . . .), well, wd have a time getting
bearings. I wd take it: a yng man: wd best, in spite of the snobs, wd
best: sit down with Lawrence: to see exactly, what CAN drive a man,
into 'extended discussion'; or for love & NO money: Stein (the early
work) & perhaps: some of the Anderson: sd pick up the Williams: for
the love of clean words & sharpness: sd read Gide: for how many sides
of the coin THERE ARE; sd take Mann & the Magic Mt (or better,
perhaps, some of the stories, for a sense of 'growth' in subject): sd get
Faulkner & forget abt F. Scott. Sd look, each time: for the SINGLE
intelligence: making its way: and should give old man Tolstoi one good
hell of a kick: out the window: we forget: that WAR & PEACE has cost
us plenty. Not a damn thing in T/ that hasn't been done a hell of a lot
cleaner in Stendhal. Well, take it: what can push a yng man to a grip of
his own: is example, others, fighting alone, etc. It is damn important
that he find them: before he's smothered in ways & means: the
'critical' intelligence. He wd have to learn the very quixote character of
any man who HAS to write a novel, etc., prose. Who IS 'wrong from
the start':[61] becuz he cant, ever, catch up: and why precisely: he
throws a whole life: into a frame of words: that will never get there.
Or WHERE he intends it to go. A contention: a novel, any novel, is a
necessary failure, and in that: is all its value. A poem can 'succeed,'
etc. But not a novel. I think here of Dos/ end of The Idiot: what Gide
has called/ for the yng reader/[62] but the 'good Russian cry' over 'this

fellow'.... as wd come at the end of any novel worth its salt. Christ: a novel is weeping for men: always. And: behind them.

Again & again, the Dr's: 'Why do I write today . . .'

Do you remember the opening of The Scarlet Letter: there H/ was writing PROSE. Sometimes: it is the jockeying for position that is 'more to the point': than what comes after it has, supposedly, been got. The 'ear' in prose: much more subtle/ well, an overstatement/ but we sd give over, at times, the kind of insistencies Ez drives to/ and pick up here and there/ on sounds. Gide et al., are off their rockers: of course: to put the weight on Cain, etc., for what they think is there: what IS there: again: a method, or in C/ case: an ear. But better/ much better/ in Faulkner. I wd never get tired of reading that 'method' in F/ & damn, usually, what he's up to/ tho many times/ the real thing. And to get to yr own biz/ how did Herman make those SOUNDS: and how in Christ's name did he drive that fustian: full steam: the works. The head & the heart. And if a man has an ear/ he can stretch the 'setting' all he's a mind to. 'No such thing as common speech.' I wd put Pierre against any of the James: to show what J/ lacked, since HM was certainly NOT making the context in P/ : BUT still going like mad. You cannot kill: anything: if you have that grip/ but lacking it: the stuff dates like/ that lady's dress. I think here of that stuff Ez was selling 30 long yrs ago: Dubliners/ & go back to that now: it's getting old & beginning to look: a little tired. But Herman? IN HIS CRIB.

Well, not the way of putting it, or any of this; casting abt etc. Was reading a yr ago/ abt this time/ Don Quixote/ and riding along with it/ Unamuno's text on same: and, perhaps, blushing, but dammit, NO : it's the way. Have looked abt for U/s works, and hard to get the novels, & have failed myself. Anyhow, that's the prose/ that & ole S[tendhal]: 'As an honourable man who abhors exaggeration, I do not know what to do . . .': losing the heart/ while keeping the head . . . The only way.

I wd look to: in prose, not only what you have put down, rightly, as a shaking up of context, and let me date here, after E/s fashion, let me date yr own entrance: as a good shaking up of myself, & for that you have all my gratitude: it is easy, too easy, to sit down.

'What the age demanded . . . the age demanded an image
of its accelerated grimace . . .

Not, not certainly, the obscure reveries
of the inward gaze . . .'[63]

Etc. I wd look to: deeper/firmer grips on content: which wd come to yr own
demands. Wd look for, again, even 'love.' It is a craft.

'Wise money wears Michigan plates . . .'

So it wd go.

[Washington, D.C.]
tuesday   may 30   L

((have come in from sittin with constanza lookin at the jungle of our garden,
the hidden garden which lured us to live here, hidden, that is, as right
rapture in this Dead City, like a rose among the broken bottles of the freight
yd behind (where the negroes go to drink, the Live Ones)

have come in, to say, last night, rereading you on the novel, it
occurred to me to offer you this flying notion—(it lies, i'd imagine,
behind my emphasis on document)

are we not automatic, to think,
that because prose-and-the-novel did, since the 18th, & conspicuously,
in the 19th, &, as you accurately note, dyingly, in the 20th, do a major
job, that it need now be fruitful?

with no arrogation, merely to go with the nose, i should take
verse as returned once more to the kind of majority it occupied in, say,
Sumer thru Homer, and again with England, and Elizabeth

and it would be my guess that, when this happens, the empire of prose shrinks, withdraws from the fictive, with no necessary loss of its potency, merely a change of the area where it best asserts its power

if, i say, the energy that good men are now putting into the nuvvel, even where they extend its technologicals, were given to the recording of the huge events unwrapping each of us

(as Rousset, e.g., wrote l'Univers Concentrationaire (not Les Jours de Notre Mort)—and, over a weekend, because he figured to die the next week of the Causes; or Martin-Chauffier, who had been a novelist, & who chose, in L'Homme et La Bete, to tell not even what he had heard others say (the last vestige of the novelist! or of the *Cantos!*) but only & precisely what had happened to him; vide Joe Gould . . .)[64]

((the small life, today, is become parabolic))

(((et les americains are the fron-tiersmen of l'univers concentrationnaire)))

Herodotus wld be come again! Or Athenaeus. Or Diogenes Laertius. Or Zenophon-Plato, writing the life of present Fact, Socrates.[65]

Anyhow, I imagine such prose as Carl O. Sauer, my friend Graham the physiopsychologist,[66] der Kulturmorphologist, F[robenius] (even Miss Benedict, who had been a poet, and turned to the recording of Cochiti tales),[67] etc., such, are too much, for novelists to match

(when poets are once more moralists and pedagogues from which they will, inevitably, become narrators)

Offered up, to you, who seek, "ways," in prose: the SINGLE INTEL-LIGENCE is, the documentor, now?

)poets, are the weepers, &
the sweepers(

have asked MONTEVALLO REVIEW to send you #1:
note, in it, & tell me, is not LIFEBOAT worth, the rest of the
prose[68]

((((on Unamuno, agree: only, the parabolic must be fastened down,
like a tent stake, if
we are to be, parabola

olson

[*In ink:*]
is, from you,
"*Wise money wears Michicayn plates*" ?

(reminds me, Ford's
argument, headlines
are now the
equivalent of
the Latin poets'
disciplines!

Also, Ford, 1938:
quoting W[yndham] L[ewis],
agin
progression d'effets, etc:

Wot's
the good of being an author
if you don't perform
like a dog on tight ropes,
and if you don't
get any fun out of it?
Efface yrself? Bilge![69]

[Littleton, N.H.]
5/31/50
Wednesday/ noon

Dear Olson,
          Very good to have these things from you: the 2 letters.
          Well: 'too much.' A coincidence that made its mark: that abt
all the close friends thru the college yrs, and later: were musicians or
were making sounds, etc. It was a shortcut to speech, understanding,
to make use of the words running with same/ or: the worst, crazy, too
much, gone, the thing, goofed, in his crib, dig, etc., etc. I.e., had lived
for about a yr, right there, and was talking most of the time/ with that
lang. Used to sit/ from abt 1 to 5 in the morning on the doorsteps, in
Boston, Columbus Avenue, talking/ watching it get light, over the
houses. Was selling a little charge/ shit/ tea/ hemp/ et al.: to victims
now & again, and wd ride abt in big cars: abt the city, hither & yon:
sometimes to Providence: North Main Street: & once, per exemplum,
was riding with a boy abt 35, & three of my own: went wrong way on a
one way St/ stopped: cop looks in & laughs: says: you boys are from
Columbus Ave: when did you get out/ shocked faces: OUT???. He
says: no one lives there without a record, etc. And later out to the track
to eat in the places the handlers have/ usually a house/ rotates, take
turns with the cooking/ and parts where the colored live: in the city: all
dirt roads/ and the main street: railroad Station/ abt 25 blocks away.
Disgust on the part of one lad: who had come from there: look at em:
like PIGS . . .   That much gone by with, like they say, here. But let's
give it another slant. There's a story abt Cocteau & the Vogue
photographers: i.e., he had a bunch of stuff for props/ at his place/ and
they came in dragging their own, and when they started to set things
up/ apparently one wanted to make use of all of it: shall we say: a great
deal, etc. Anyhow: Cocteau says no ..... a *little* too much is enough
for me .....   You will see: the same thing.

Of course: for ways in speech, sounds & timing: there is nobody like,
say, the colored: negroes: a rhythm & a feel for each thing that comes
out of their mouths. That wd take some time to document, like they
also say.

Well, abt the bit having to do with that from the past letter. [*Added in margin:* the gloss] Up to you: sounds too much, but make sure you want it there, & not only: just delight/ or what you will/ that I had got at least some of it. But as you will; certainly, it wd be fun.

I write poetry & prose, like they say. Had meant to send you some of both, and will, one of these days, when I get to it. Not important at the time/ or now. I'm not up to the things I've seen in yr own work, but still: fair enough that you should judge for yrself.

You'll have the biz re prose: & will take it from that: that I am yr man: on Lawrence, & D[ostoevski]. I had looked at this in Blake yesterday: Nature has no Outline, but Imagination has/[70] & wd that not be: the basic to judging the passage from INformal to FORmal. We have so fucked up the sense of 'form' that all that comes into it suffers as well/ or in this case: the above 2 words. And since things are what they are, etc. : for the time, take it: form is the outline of the imagination/ on what it takes to hand. I dont know that I cn take it: as INformal/ or take that, rather, as the basis for an effort/ in poetry, etc. You know enough abt what I wd say: to judge that this has nothing to do with an approval of yr own insistence/ or the Projective Verse. The 'formal' has killed what the head: might get into: in that it has put into menial/ enclosed/ work: what it sd have been determining, ONLY, as an extension of its center: in any given work. Which is to say: as now, in many, the insistence on an attention (FIRST) to possible castings for a content: has belied the content: or no more than the Dr's implication re the suitability of the sonnet/ for our time, etc.[71] Of a piece: it has to be. Exercises : sd determine the grip on either form or content: but neither sd usurp. And much that seems to me/ as being at the root of yr own view: is the matter of one's own stake in the content: or what cd serve as reason: for wanting to have it round: like sound: and full.

Foolish: to make limits: that dont come from what's being talked abt directly, or in this case: I lack the grounding of examples. Or am too lazy to put them in.

Abt prose & howin it might differ, in use, in what it cd get to: from poetry. The main thing: the distance in prose, that to be taken as, the

possible reach between writer/content/reader: is a bigger & more
tenuous thing: to mean: the compression of poetry, must smack of the
single intelligence: must be deadcenter under the will. The drift: in
prose, like what the sailor wd allow for: is important. Almost like a net/
and too: the shiftings. And relapses/ and slips. (An aside: a man is
much less apt to 'know' what he is talking abt in prose than he is in
poetry.) I.e., where cd this statement/ comment: fit in poetry: 'If it
ever happens to me to invent another story, I shall allow only
well-tempered characters to inhabit it—characters that life instead of
blunting, sharpens. Laura, Douviers, La Perouse, Azais . . . what is to
be done with such people as these? It was not I who sought them out;
while following Bernard and Oliver I found them in my path. So much
the worse for me; henceforth it is my duty to attend them.'[72]

That is one of the main things/ wherein: the difference.

Abt EP/ very hard for me to tell: just how much of it is DP. Anyhow,
cant expect them to do more than this: BUT can they expect me to take
it seriously, or much of it. The rub. But not a very great matter: either
way.

I think if we first get to the single aspect of any work we might do: this
to have only to do with poetry or prose (and the magazine forgotten for
the moment): I think in short: if we make it the Doc's way: which even
as you have said: means he has to be passed/ or put aside: for what we
can do/ and not we: but each/ and no point in a possible 'getting
together' .... the thing: the absolute singleness which must be for any
union to ever be/ between anything & anything else. Strip & make
clean. EP: wants a union before those involved have centered
themselves. & this is dangerous. I cant go with it.

What drivel . . .

Anyhow, will tuck in a letter from Leed here. He's a good boy. What I
owe to him, etc. I think he has it right: he mistakes, tho, my insistence
on going on: to mean I've been advertising it as something to run for
100 & 1000 of yrs, etc. He's right: i.e., best to center on the education/

and make that clear: for a series of issues/ and then go on: with what we've picked up in experience, etc. Just he loses: it's very hard to keep the thing capped/ tho it must be. Witness: letter from toujour a toi/ [Dallam] Simpson: saying MEET ME IN NYC/ MID JUNE. (if my shoes hold out, perhaps . . .)   But anyhow, like another man wrote today: wd you do a critique of my COLLEGE . . .   good lord, I have to keep things cool, and one way is, to plot a length, that wd allow for all that might bear/ and wd, too, have the virtue, of allowing the pressures to cool, in the process. But so much for that. Take it: I think he has it right: for immediate plans, and think too: my letters to you re this: have been in this vein. You might check me/ there/ to see if I have made it straight: and haven't as he said: NOT hit the difficulties of inexperience & getting a center to carry us, till we know abt the biz.

Will write soon again/

and you do the same.

All best,
Creeley

Again abt the PRO gig/ as you will: but tell me if you do/ so I can get a copy to my mother ....

Wish to Christ I cd get down to yr town, etc. To see & see, too, the Lawrence: the nearest I'd come: a large portfolio of reproductions (my bitter lot in this life. . . ah. . .), but had the gist.[73] Go back to the books many times, for what might push me. Or what pushed him. Had hit this in an excerpt from some of his letters to Bertrand Russell:

'The repeating of a known reaction upon myself is sensationalism . . .'
Elsewhere: 'I cannot help Prometheus. And this knowledge rots the love of activity . . .'[74]

[*Added at top of letter:*] Abt: Kitasono/ lack a set of 4PP at the moment, loan/ but will get it back & see what's up there. Thanks.

[Washington, D.C.]
wed.   may 31   L

suspicion:

that FRANCIS THOMPSON[75]

is very much
of USE

o   el   ess   o   enn

[*verso:*]
QUATRAIN

Do not, at this high time, desert
(from pain, distraction, of the mind, of the senses, of
believing

the raising up—we are all, we are all, forever
lone-ing

that raising up which is, forever is, the will
of our own self-ing
desert not, here at the Bloody Angle, where even death may be,
the Cause, the Cause, it is
the cause!

[Littleton, N.H.]
thur/ june 1, 50

Dear O,

　　　fair enough: that you sd call it 'automatic,' since that is the usual method of assumption/ and the way: is the result of a stasis: in apprehension of possible method. But I have to put it: impossible not to attempt the variety of media: that might fall to hand. But as yrself: have doubts as to whether or not/ prose can keep pace with 'present developments,' since in some ways it comes to that. Again: the compression & push of poetry: toward a single 'action' of comprehension: is damn attractive for a time, that has no anchor, and even, wants none. Because/ in some sense certainly: the novel came out of: ruminations: or a time for such, granted it had been written, too, in times such as these. I expect I am thinking only of Fielding, etc. Certainly, Dos/ & Stendhal were bucking the wave. Hence, the above is invalid. Well, how to put it, this attraction, not for the 'novel,' but better: for possible prose. IT FALLS TO HAND: this is important. To make use, if possible, of what best goes with yr thinking. Yr own method of apprehension. Just as I cannot write yr poetry, I have to fight the good fight: alone. It may be, certainly, that the effort will be nil/ but how in hell does that come into it? Yes, not a novel abt: that I can call center. Or it. [John] Hawkes' effort/ well, not it. A grip, certainly, but not kept hold of. So much for that. He had told me: my life & my art: have nothing to [do] with one another. Which belies him: but which he still tries to maintain. At least, a poetry: wd make it 'personal.'

The 'Wise money wears Michigan plates' was from Cain[76]/ and had put it in there/ god knows why. Take it: a good instance of how to make an aphorism. All the grounding. If a prose cd stick to that tone: it wd be closer. One thing that had always made me like Faulkner: was the insistence on what was under hand/ as he found it. I.e., what a slush of random hearsay: Sartre is. Much closer: Camus' The Stranger, as I wd put it against his Plague, which leaves me not a little: bored.

The provincial: which plagues me/ as you will note when you see the
story, etc., is not easily shaken. I haven't yr grip on what is unfolding/
and cant trust myself: to that which I cannot grab hold of: at least in
some way. This is why: you had my mouth/open YES: on La Preface.
That's what I wd say: wd be it . . . Yet, is it not (to use an Olson) nice:
to see the Old Man/ drifting in the Cantos: according to his bent
. . .   ruminator & it was always MY way . . .   History of ONE
man, in spite of, and because of: the references. And what the hell is
history/ except the mind that can contain it . . .   Shit. And what is it:
then.

The Dr did nothing with stories—*Am G[rain]* something else again:
but to keep it clean. And to document, further, how close it might get
to its surroundings. But in that: he never did more than look at it/ no
transformations. Have to go back: to get to them. Who were TELLING
the stories, and be damned: to what had happened.

Abt Kitasono. One can respect this thing. I cant go much farther, damn
me, as you will. It has all the 'conjecture' for the tightening, and dont
mistake me to mean: conclusion. It is that passage from what is
pushing in the poem, to its being effected in the bite & rhythm of the
words: to drag you on & on. Power. That this lacks, except as
potential. Damn it: I miss something there/ that cd have put it sharper.
And this is NOT words only, but it is the relation between you & what
you're writing abt. I get the statement, god knows: of this horror, and
isn't it: yes: it is familiar. I lack what? Like this:

> I that in heill was and gladness
> Am trublit now with great sickness
> And feblit with infirmitie: —
>   *Timor mortis conturbat me.*[77]

Almost: let's call em straight.

But shit, it's not it: that, to put on the other. I just miss the bite of all
the head: on what is under hand. Let me go back to it.

Robert Creeley with his wife Ann and son David in Littleton, New Hampshire, 1950. Charles Olson Collection. Literary Archives, University of Connecticut Library.

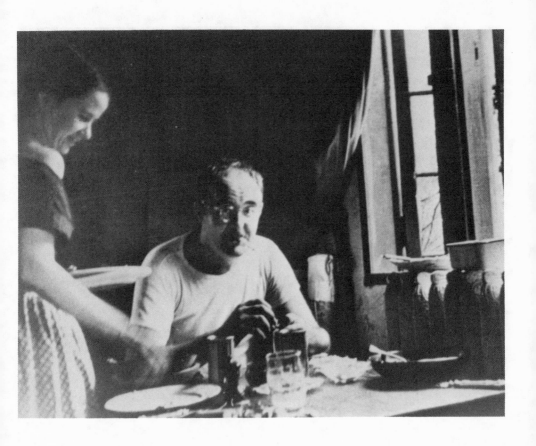

Charles Olson with his wife Constance in Washington, Spring 1950.
Photograph by Marc Ribaud, courtesy of Jean Ribaud. Charles Olson
Collection. Literary Archives, University of Connecticut Library.

set/

Dear O,

and why not a little sugar/ by way of an opening/ And why
not: 'Poems by Olson were... too much... Cannot believe him,
it is so rare that he is all one might say... For he does
write so very great...' From Z. Baron/ so not in vain. Etc.

Other things: today along with yr own/ a letter from Gordon
Ringer/ who I think may be a boy for the education whirl//
has the head & the motives & the facts. Willing: and hope
he can put it down. Useless to say: what: until I see what
he turns in. Also today the letters, etc. back from EP:
(and had included yr own THE MORNING NEWS & MOVE OVER to
show him what I took to be of use, etc.) with this note by
his right hand/ DF: 'E.P. much too exhausted to advise on
ms/ and in any case has been long convinced that no one can
usefully do this for the generations that come after him...'
Ho Ho. And what have you been up to/ old sport/ and what was
that abt: 'fatuity...'??? What is this wife like, he has? Who
takes that tone with ME, DAMMIT??? O well: a joke. And put
against the constant hand/holding of the past 3 months/ a good
joke. At least she quotes him on Leed: 'He finds your printer
'simpatico'.'

Of course: time/ comes to push off from that particular shore.
For whatever.

The only possible 'reforming' cd be done in 2 ways: what EP had
called that category of criticism which meant: in new composition,

Robert Creeley letter to Charles Olson, 27 May 1950. Charles Olson
Collection. Literary Archives, University of Connecticut Library.

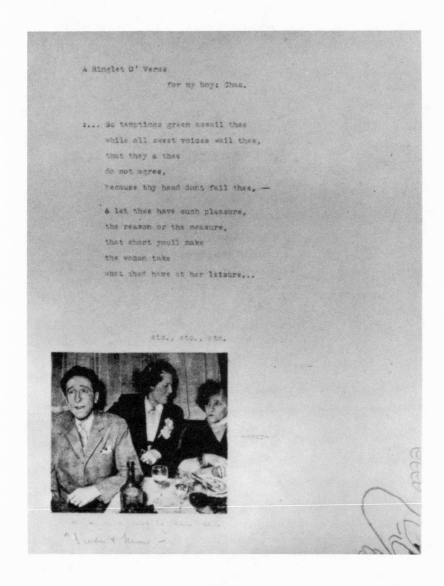

Section of Robert Creeley's letter to Charles Olson, 1 June 1950. Photograph clipped from newspaper includes Cocteau and Colette. Charles Olson Collection. Literary Archives, University of Connecticut Library.

I wanna be GOOFED but only by pot.   June 17

C. Parker, looking at a photograph of himself at the age of 6:
            'I was a clean little bird then...'

                    when yez be in NE???

Dear O,

        A difficult thing (you send me) to write abt. To take
it round the back way, etc. Where you come best: is where you
center/ make around: a thing as tangible as THIS. I.e., we
get here/ beauty...(& cd best say, perhaps,: is still (still)
difficult, or: here, I find it hard to see by way of the document.) I dislike (I dont like at all) the going back to MOVE
OVER and LA PREFACE, etc. BUT, but, we had the center of yrself there, most certainly. I cant get the corpus here/ the
body or the heart/ more than what I am 'told' and I am a hard
one, to believe. I/ here, that is 'I' is NOT the eye in MOVE
over, the looker/ who sees with force, but is, instead, rambler.
That is, the difficulty, as a reader wd judge it, of yr style,
is to maintain a logos, a power of method, derived from (form)
(from content)/ that lays bare: yr center, or: of what use the
document, IF: no final stripping, can be effected. You say that
yrself/ to yrself. I serve no function here.

But this is hard on what's good there, and much of that, tho:
I miss the tightness of the others, & the sweep. What had pushed
you in IN COLD HELL, etc., what has to push you, if you can be
pushed, and you can, etc. (The 1st 2 lines of 3, I like.)
Also of II/ but too close to: the surface/ glances: off. Where
it should: dig in.

                Well, fuck it. You do better. Impossible
to like them all, or it would be possible. Always: the way,
certainly.

Robert Creeley letter to Charles Olson, 17 June 1950. Charles Olson
Collection. Literary Archives, University of Connecticut Library.

p.s. - wrote R. Emerson today, to say *what about the olson anthology for 66 #2, (which would be 2-3-4 months after his retiring early fall; + I thank him for welcoming me, via Creeley, yes, the Kingfisher, & Cole Hall. Did not yet send my de'r c:*

        friday june 23 50

my de'r c:

       i never drew, on hart/don't know why/his life, yes, like him, special it's of no importance, no measure whatsoever, but the verse, never did invoke me (tempted to think, simply because, feel so close to, the man (queer, that way: never did, on HM, either, or lawrence, draw: just like 'em, like to think abt 'em, now: seems like, i go around collecting brothers, or whateverImaseem, in lieu of having same) (anyhow, awful ignorant, abt other writers: somehow resist influence, except for those I mentioned to you yesterday)

       sure you're right on hart, for yrself (rather question, tho, relation hart-melville: if xx i had a demur on h c, i think it wld be, that, when he was, it was too late for America: already the body of this land was crocked And her seas)

       Did do, come to think of it, a verse on hart! the lst days i ever did same And it xxxxx caused the most enigmatic business, between me and Marsden Hartley I was heart-broken, for Hartley had found out my address on Christopher St (god, what a darling of a one-room house, with parquet-soapstoned floor, and me alone, for the lst time in my life, trying to go to the mat with same) and, to my honor & surprise, come to see me in a new beautiful sea-green suit he'd bought, where I used to buy mine, my Harrises, at Macy's Made-To-Measure, 35 bucks! There he was, at my door! It was his peak, the lst or 2nd Walker show, after his extraordinary 2nd birth (at 50, or so), the return to Maine. And I was his. I was so nervous, I made tea, but it was only orange slices in hot water, I had forgotten to add the tea, and didn't know it, the cups were red 'erican clay, until he had gone. It went all right, until I pulled out, in my green enthusiasm, the Hart poem. He read it, slowl, sd no word, got up, took his hat, and walked out!

       It has bothered me, since that day. Damned if I know, what went on. I still suffer over it.

       Anyhow, what i wanted to say was, I called hart, new archeopteryx. And do have that feeling, that he was somehow some marvelous throw-back, a vestigia, forward, in that sense, surely.

       Agree, eloquent, as HM was, but think what you so accurately put, embarassment, (& Bill also), (causeth) is actually that, what is the JOB, is to find a method (a logos, is it also to be called) OTHER THAN THE ELIZABETHAN, and what embarasseth (Ezra, never) is the Elizabethan in

         melville, hart, & bill, sometimes, not very many times

(dry it out, bboys, dry it out!)
((go to sea, citizens,
        and find out))
{{((Amb was FULL STOP: yr enemies, (how did you spell it?), are done for, and all the 1c way: the ENERGY Malaysourny
   is elsewhere)))
       and where it is,
            is for us to find, for the likes

you and me, POET, grandson of, CHAMP PETIE!
       Signed Olson, one - Dom

"To one of but who stay, jump, yes, You who makes a bridge / leaps to

Anyhow, will put some poems in here/ I cant do it either/ but know what has to be done.

Put this away for now.

Be strong.

Creeley

or even this: bless my sentimental sool, etc.

'The sentence undulates
raising no song—
It is too old, the
words of it are falling
apart. Only percussion
strokes continue
with weakening
emphasis what was once
cadenced melody
full of sweet breath.'

. . . is Creeley: 'there never
was another more another than
this one . . . !

More of same:[78]

'What am I, said Leo, twenty-six, almost twenty-seven, and I am in good health and have many years to do with as best I can . . .'

'You could push him to the end of desire, like they say, that being not so far as is supposed, and a quiet place, relaxed, and more than most, comfortable. Sickness didn't mean that he was dead . . .'

'Like that, he said, that I was then thinking of it, the beer. That was what I had in mind. And I could love that too, I expect. One thinks of the hot days and it's not so hard then.

She said: but not the same way.

The same way, he said, no different . . .'

'We say that what lives enjoys particularity, being separate, apart in a way that is unmistakable. Down the streets are the entities, beings of irregular purpose who live, as it were, in a condition of this kind, neither wanting nor demanding an order that forces alikeness. And why this is cannot be quite determined or if it can be explained, of what use is the explanation, the catching up, beside the wonder of the things themselves. But beyond all this, into the disparate worlds of existence, say that there live others, perhaps as yet not apprehended, however particular their lives . . . Can it be, then, that there are really other things to consider? . . . But to come from this into the descendant nightmare of love, who will forgive me for that . . .'

A Ringlet O' Verse

for my boy: Chas.

: . . . So temptings green assail thee
while all sweet voices wail thee,
that they & thee
do not agree,
because thy head dont fail thee,   —

& let thee have such pleasure,
the reason or the measure,
that short youll make
the woman take
what shed have at her leisure . . .

etc., etc., etc.

[*Photograph of Cocteau and Colette:*]

And O/ says prose is dead. Heh. [*Added in pencil by Creeley:* "I wdn't know—]

Still Life Or

> mobiles: that the wind can
> catch at, against itself, a
> leaf or a contrivance of
> wires, in the stairwell, to
> be looked at from below.
>
> We have arranged the form
> of a formula here, have
> taken the heart out, and
> the wind is vague emotion.
>
> To count on these aspirants,
> these contenders for the
> to-be-looked-at part of
> these actions, these most
> hopeful movements, needs
> a strong & constant wind.
>
> That will not rise above
> the speed which we have
> calculated, that the leaf
> remain, that the wires
> be not too much shaken.

Ira

> or
> the firm hand of
> love.
>
> The family—
>   falling apart—
> went bad

        & rotten at the center.
But hung around
to plague the old man.

The old man.
Old clothes & a mustache
will make still
the happy man.

Ira: a fine man, abt 71; & we make the shows together: poultry. A
Christ-like myopia, he is blessed with.

The Epic Expands

        They had come in a carriage (which
will be less than what's needed)
over the hard roads. And they stop
in the town to get coke, three
bottles, by way of a celebration.

So will the epic expand (or be
expanded by) its content. So will
words throw (throw up) their meaning.
Words they have used (will use) are
the sound (of sound), what gets us.

But to go farther (he could not
stop there), to look at the old
people, graceless and cold, in a
carriage with (say) one blanket
between them, to keep out the cold—

and it was, he said (he said), it
was a coldness of the mind, too (too).

Yes, poets, we had overlooked an
essence, and, quiet (put back into
quiet), we let the tears roll down.

The Primitives
Poem from a Photograph: East African Natives[79]

1.

All in a picture,
collected by the artist
and told to be
quiet, they were.

There are seven
in all and the faces
are no less than
fourteen eyes

which look out at
the one who is looking
in. In back are
their houses.

But for the one,
it will be a test of
seeing that he
is being seen.

2.

I expect that they
are people but I do not
know. It is
yet to be seen.

What their faces seem
is my own way of looking
and the light is
almost too flat.

In this relation
I am somewhat thankful
that they are not
an archaic white—

even remembering
that some sallow yellow,
however usual,
would be worse.

3.

Not to be argued
that we see these things
in rare settings,
it is a fact.

The new is the new.
Not always the unwanted,
it says only what
it wants to say

and we listen, or
not, as we think best.
What we can argue
depends on what

we know. So, too,
with these irrefutable others,
notwithstanding
the very odd look.

A Local Celebration

> With the sun coming in
> over the window and even
> the least edge, the least
> of it bright, a dazzle,
> what is there more of
> brightness or of signs
> of brightness or of
> eyes seeing brightness?
>
> Because you catch me with
> your sadness, and you love
> me, the sun should be
> as bright, should be
> brighter, for you, and
> tears—a kind of edge for
> the sun to catch on in
> its indeterminate despair.

Song: 'Rough Winds Doe Shake The Darling Of My Heart'

> (let's say: fer Ez: with apologies to Louis
> Simpson, etc., etc., etc.)[80]

Rough winds doe shake
                    doe shake
                              the darling of my heart.
This darling heart
              my heart
                    these winds doe shake.

To be my part,
A fart, these winds, rough winds, her winds doe make.

She is unkind
                unkind
                        and her young bum
Is like a horn
            loud horn
                    a vivid brass
Her arse become.
Upon this horn she blows till all the neighbors wake.

Her bum will break
                will break
                        unless I can
Let loose the flow
            foul flow
                    for my own sake.
For she is torn
Between these sighs, and those, from me, she'd take.

Yet am I lost
            all lost
                    to all my heart.
So doth she fart
            long fart
                    and I am toss't.
The bed's apart.
In pieces, too, my heart. Her fart, all it did break.

Er . . .
EP's gloss is helpful here: 'Only grrrrreat clarity cn cut thru . . .'

By this HERE hand: this 1st day of
JUNE: this nineteenth & 50th: yr, by
hundreds. Good lord.

Creeley

[Littleton, N.H.]
Monday/ june 5 [1950]

Dear O,

Blood from a stone and all that sort of thing/ USELESS to kick
against the pricks, i.e. : 'If it were at any other time of the year we
could send you an advance check for the story. But the Summer issue is
the last of our fiscal year, and our comptroller, the College Treasurer,
has imposed it as a rigid rule that we cannot make advances for material
that may appear in the following fiscal year, etc., etc . . .'

'Consideration of your account will be appreciated. If your check has
been mailed, please accept out thanks . . .'

Well, subjectivity, etc. For my money/ never was: else. I.e., take it, or
not (little matter): that concurrent with the 'deliberatism' of 'science':
came the supposition: that a 'cool head' needed an explicit tag. A
disastrous split, nonetheless; and opposition on this head: altogether
useless & a waste of precious time. No such thing as 'objectivity' for
the man who wants to do a good job. Or . . .

Will pick up: on this comment: since it's a center. I.e., 'a man must create himself . . .' [*Added in margin:* (looking back, I see I misread you—it is: "man must create himself—instrument—"[81] Still, my first reading is—close enough (ha!).] I wd say so: and more, that it is the possible variations on the center/creation: that make up the plot of art, granted its center is: what you say. Or as they used to say: the foci & the loci, etc. Or words to that effect. We are NOT mathematicians/ or we are: and then some. Breaking down the supposition/ that prose & poetry: depend on perhaps counter/ at least 'different' kinds of attitude & intelligence: we can get to the agreement you take to exist: in the use of both: of the S.I. The need. Again: what posits A as A, is the existence of B/ no MATTER: if it 'exist' . . . It is the variation: that can accomplish its status in the sense of: A. I see no need for MORE than ONE head: if it's a good one. Or better: I can not see that such a head: should feel that OTHERS were essential. This is to break down: the supposition: that we are first & foremost: a continuum.

Abt 'myth' & the Kollektif Basket: the talking ABT myth: it wd seem to me: works to destroy the essential feature/ pervasiveness MINUS exact root/ or 'in the air' like they say. Now, granted the 'use,' valid or otherwise, to which it has been put/ as a 'name' for a body of 'information'/ as an insight into past or existing 'group' intelligence . . . [*Added by Creeley in margin:* blah.] It seems only: when it can be used/ as a manifestation of its own character: that it has valid testament. To be such: it must again become: pervasive & unidentified. Here/ of course: myth : IS in the air/ and none to do more than MAKE USE OF it in reasoning/ in apprehension of what might be around. (This is way off the beat, etc . . . [*Added in margin:* I dont know shit abt any of this—]

Again: abt 'instruments . . .' ('becoz he is instrument, & uses all available instruments only to dominate 'em, not his fellow cits . . .'): you will know of all the blah: abt possible 'audiences' in the case of both prose & poetry/ you will also know: absolute bull/shit. That is: the intelligence that had touted Auden as being a technical wonder, etc. Lacking all grip on the worn & useless character of his essence: thought. An attitude that puts weight, *first:* on form/ more than to say: what you have above: will never get to: content. Never in god's

world. Anyhow, form has now become so useless a term/ that I blush
to use it. I wd imply a little of Stevens' use (the things created *in* a
poem and existing there . . .)[82] & too, go over into: the possible casts
or methods for a way into/ a 'subject': to make it clear: that form is
never more than an *extension* of content.[83] An enacted or possible
'stasis' for thought. Means to.

Abt the Uni/s, etc. Leed's poets as pedants/ to mean: the academic use
of the 'particles,' etc. carried into a raison d'etre for SONG. Or, more
precisely, the analyzers, in poetry/ who are NOT the analyzers in
poetry, etc. You see/? Well, put something down on that head/ using
Leed anyway you want. Granted, I can: that the Poet as Pedagogue/ is
the TEACHER. That, too: you had put down fully.

Take this for
now: will try to catch up soon.

Best to you,

Creeley

I had read once with delight: de Gourmont's attack on 'romanticism'
which was, praises be: a good stand for subjectivity . . . [*Added:* he
"subjected" his data—]

opener in PG's The Dead Of Spring: which has just come under the
hand, like they say:

'Friends have reached the most beautiful part of their
meeting: the impasse from which *nevertheless* they do not get up and
leave. They are resting in this hell . . .'
Then he begins to 'chew' . . . .[84]

[*Added:*] Vol. 2—Del Mar—[85]*also* here this 5th day of June—

Was thinking if, perhaps, Wasserman,[86] et al.—had not provided the
"transition" from Dostoyevsky—to the social observer—   others as
well (it was that 'way')

Some more abt the poets being the only pedagogues// at this point, or at
this stage of the game: the only possible pedagogues. I take this in the
sense of/ 'science of teaching' (flat phrase) or better: those capable of
demonstrating, thru USE: a method, a way: of transmitting:
communicating: idea/thought/ 'history,' etc.

Leed's thought: only to do with a related word/ coming only from the
pedagogue's MISuse of his calling, etc. Pedantry/ many poets now ARE
pedants, or they have been put to the same dry work of evolving
superficials, for already assumed, often already completed: analysis,
etc. Again: an instance of having made the way/ the end. Well: do such
need any kind of attention. A hard thing to comment on; IF one is busy
with one's own work (and be damned, and rightly, to the MISuse of
others . . .). A pounder/ wd know this/ as did he: constantly reiterate
the dreariness of talking ABT aht, etc. It comes to/ how far do you take
the current pedantry in poetry to block: understanding & development
of same/ how great do you take the damage, if any, to be: to what the
Dr. called 'means to leap the gap . . .'. That they are: the
'nonpurveyors' . . .[87] one wd take that as fact. That one's work sd
be concerned with their failure/ well, that's the question . . . If one can
shake free, fair enough that he should: certainly . . . But very damn
hard to find room, these days . . . free of them, or their thought, or
their damned rigidity, and ugliness. Hence: the magazine: first—the
point wd be, or better: cd be: to cast light on: illumine: make available
: aspects of the universities: not taken seriously, or not usually seen to
be harmful. Some months ago, re this whole thing, Bud had written: I
hate to think of you as 'clearing the air' rather than trying to give: 'a
new substance . . .' Beyond my capabilities to do either: it's the pivot
round which one's actions, in such matters: can swing, or loop. Or just
damn well droop. That is, I grant you, certainly, yr own good reasons
for not seeing (I have to assume this, at this point . . .) how effectual
Leed's slant can be/ put against yr own idea of the poets as pedagogues/
one, the first, being against, and the second, yrs, moving at least to a:
projection, a positivism: of attitude. Having thought much, like they
say, abt these matters, and the limits best set/ for a first launching,
etc.: I had to take the fact, that very damn few wd be willing to come to
a demonstration of yr own statement. Obviously, the point is NOT to
come to something ABT it, but rather: to make it, actual, in the corpus

of yr work. Well, the dead wood/ and the lack of guts, and the general hate & fear: of what a poetry, a prose: cd grip/ given the center: just, dammit, plain suspicion: having only to do with the 'possible' pride a man might feel: IF he were capable, actually, of more than ruminations . . . for these it must be: well, you had yr Lawrence & you had yr Pound/ and a few others: and they cd never agree among themselves/ and all they were: was arrogant, and, at last: we couldn't understand a damn thing they said . . . And, if for example, either Lawrence or Pound had had: an educational system going full steam: to back THEM up??? The point: a certain am't of clearing has to be done/ and it matters not that much: what or who does it/ so long as it's done . . . A magazine, or anything, with a reader potential: has the chance: and I will make use of it. But not RIDE it to death, or anywhere similar.

This is obtuse/ and I hate to beg off, each time I get to where I sd be hitting the point. Somewhere (back) it's in there, but to weed it out/ cant do it: now. Or at this moment.

Well, hitting something, elsewhere: it is simple enough to take the law, of S.I., if you will: as bearing on both aspects of the word. I wd transpose one or two words here & there, only for purposes of my own coherence: say . . . 'illumination . . .' vs. 'expression' as you had it there. Wd become for myself: (expression) the line running

off.

And (illumination) the line: running, IN STASIS . . . which means no more than it: is held, in tension, the line of the intelligence as manifest by its expression: in 'words,' material, or has: more simply: posited itself as 'complete' in an 'example.'

That given: you have the basis for a distinction between good & bad prose/// the difference coming to, what is a 'circle' in prose & what is: an 'ending . . .'

I.e., a good novel, as a good poem: CANNOT: 'conclude . . .' /// it exists/ only to be returned to.

(Obviously, here I dont give a damn with what the author cites as an 'ending' [*added:* rhetorical convention.] on pp 250-255., etc.)

Sd not think that language, per se, wd have any more reality than Blake's Nature/ it is the Imagination which has Outline . . . or better, that which defines: the real. In its first aspect.

This is the bulwark of 'romanticism' they say, but that argument is fruitless.

Again: very much wish that it were possible to see you. That is, the impossible time/lag in mail, etc. Well, no ultimate bug, but a nuisance. Here/ impossible to move, or to travel anywhere. No money, and damned by inconsequent possessions of one sort and another. Well: we wait only for the best time: to heave them/ tho perhaps the waiting is itself: disaster. So, during the war, while impossible to realize anything that was going on/ tho I cd see all of it with my eyes (i.e., can there be any reality in suffering of that sort, the physical, when it reaches a proportion you cannot, in any sense, imagine, etc. [*added in margin:* (i.e., the consistent: pitch of actual pain: was such: that you could not believe it: anymore than you can take it as fact: that a hen 'suffers' after you've chopped the 500th head: THO it is that consciousness: of reaction: that one MUST maintain. But the continual death, & pain/ at that point: were such that they were NOT.)]): became, like an idiocy: delight in the movements possible. The greatest possible pleasure in shuttling abt.

I pay it back, at this point.

With great vividness: Tel Aviv, which was an end in itself: a city at that point: one cd not have designed more perfectly. Or filled with such people. After having come from Burma, etc. The Am. Field Service/ which was a group of completely divers people/ having no 'head' or nothing more than one cd think of: at the moment. Truly: Fabrizio:s/[88] Anyhow, spent abt 2 weeks in Tel Aviv, after the Americans had left/ Arabs & Jews were then/ holding off. But a crazy city. Well, the freedom that cd get you on a boat/ sitting down/ two days at sea: to look out at the water & possible birds, etc. That wd be it.

The point: there are parts of Burma, villages. And people: who maintain/ a way of looking altogether distinct from our own. And while this is simple enough to talk abt/ say you are alone in such a place/ with the air abt you: only then IS IT FELT.

Trying to keep up, etc.

A note from Leed/ that he agrees: yr way in the prose bits/ the right one, i.e., : 'olson on projective and on g-pa extremely what we want . . .' He will have the stuff back to you shortly; i.e., wants to get well into it, etc. Slow but sure/ and not so slow, at that. I.e., it has to be/ a human being talking abt what he might reasonably, as evidenced by his 'style,' be supposed to have some stake in . . . etc. We wd have no use/ for the 'casual' eye, etc. The so-called: objectivist, etc. I have yet to figure: WHY in point of style, say, the heart sd be taken: as necessarily out of it: granted Kenneth Patchen aint usually: it. Still: I'd go with some of it/ seeing he can shake it up: now & again: tho I feel sad: that it sd come to so very damn little. Rather: it was Henry [Miller]: now & again: letting loose with the round-about story/ that had the right kick. Or/ 'if I call M/ Claude a whore . . . what am I going to call other women . . .'[89] Or: the long bit about the return to Brooklyn/ which has always warmed me. Better than what passes for better/ god knows. Then the 'gems'/ like they say: abt the arguing with the customs official/ which documents the incongruities of this life, etc. Or that little excursus/ The Hamlet Letters/ or death IS (not) enough???
     Then Fraenkel's kick/ jesus/ how dull can you get . . . NOT that it cdn't have been MAKE: but he sure didn't make it
. . .

     There is so very damn little to warm one, these days, or, as when once a friend was staying with us/ and I was sitting in another room reading: I heard her say to him: 'He often laughs like that, when he reads . . .'

     Or somewhere not too long ago/ I read a 'serious' comment abt the possible 'reason' for WHY EP had written: Papyrus
. . .

     Well: GONGULA.[90]

So it wd go.

Word To Live By: 'You know, if there weren't distribution expenses,
we might come close to break even . . .'

                                                    R. Leed.

Who had also sd: 'I am engaged in that worst of all possible
occupations: making money . . .'

yes: abt Francis Thompson/ had hit a bit of his in the Summer
HOPKINS REVIEW// all that I cn remember. But that fair enough.
Tho little to go on. What wd be the background/ or what can you tell
me, old sport, re these deep things:

                              I suspect . . .

hmm.   USE??? What use?

                              Just give the possible slant, & will be
glad to do the work, etc. Always on the job/ and ready to talk
chickens.

            yr old poultry friend.

                              C.

                                            [Littleton, N.H.]
                                                    6/6/6
                                            [6 June 1950]

Dear O,
        Today, amid a 'group' of 'things': from DP, a copy of VOU with
yr poem// too much.[91] What are they saying (THERE) these people
. . .? Eh. Eh bien. Who are the people in the pictures (photographs)
. . . do you know? What else: with it: R. Duncans: poems, HD/ Rilke's

trans./ cpy: NINE (1st)/ money papers/ a sheet from 'market quotes/
rural paper . . .' Good stuff,   as ever, yr lad:

                                        Creeley

                                        [Washington, D.C.]
                                        thurs. june 8   50

my excellent friend:
                        been tied up for three days (& is it not of yr
doin'?) on a thing now called "Story: Olson, & Bad Thing," which is
verse rasslin out of prose, and prose winnin, and then, verse emergin

                        otherwise you'd have heard sooner abt Creeley:
Packet of Verse for O, Ringlet, which, right off the bat provoked: o
wonderful, he, has two strings to his bow!

                        & now yr letter with at least one sentence to
make me, to, create this cit. for this day plus:

FORM IS NEVER MORE THAN AN EXTENSION OF
CONTENT,
                &, try this on,
                        right form
is the precise & correct [*typed above:* (only possible)] extension of
content under hand
                Anyhow, yrs
is beautiful, and most USABLE

                        (And, as you say, how many are:
until recently I wld shout, the americans are the poets, but, now, since
when, I'm gettin god damned fed up lookin for the equals of, in this

generation, of Bill—Ez—EE—yr Stevens—maybe Moore/ my god, take a look even at 'em, let alone the 20 odd other shits who make up that little shit Cole's CELEBRANT Imagi[92]— kee—rist, what ballless boys & girls he can pick up (only one, crews, who stopped me for a split second: & ee is a bore now, bill's 1st only makes it, miss moore is just a bad swipe of olson's material (sex [*i.e.* sez] the wife), and EZ? reawlly

PLEASE, c., tell me abt somebody beside thee & me, quick, or I shall quit this profession as I have quit all previous ones, and go out under some ridge pole in gloucester town, and sit, forever, the new buddha, under the gulls, & their much more understandable shit

but to biz.: question 1: shall i make final copy of STORY, and send along to c., just for his impressions of same, or no? [*Added in margin:* (no, not today, anyway)]

Next: the verse of, my poultry man:

two strings, and the joint was jumpin over "So temptings green assail thee" becoz, this string I didn't know, tho the other I knew fr passage in letter some time ago (to which I will come back)

now, two days later, i have to undo this nice little leader and talk abt three—if, as I think, EPIC EXPANDS, is diffrunt, at base, fr the YET UNDONE (the letter)

anyhow, let's go in ((remembering, as you'll see, if I send you STORY, olson males (me, and the old man are all i know) are weak (fr softness of the heart, i'm told—that is, me, because of the irish) in in-work!)):

lets go in, as I was sayin, let's make a picture of CREELEY, shall we?

say I (dictum): this man can I.) truly return us to the antient anglo-saxon heart (it is a form, a form!)—because? he's got a head with a long stride in it (like they used to talk abt long legs as a sign of, distinction? anyhow, he

thinks good, and the cadence of his thot is long & intricate, & thus
he must continue, or show me more of

>   . . . .So temptings green assail thee
>   while all sweet voices wail thee,
>   that they & thee
>   do not agree,
>   because thy head dont fail thee,— [*Added in margin:*
>   (beautiful!)]

>   & let thee have such pleasure,
>   the reason or the measure,
>   that short you'll make
>   the woman take
>   what shed have at her leisure . . .

[*Added in margin:*] (here's a problem: at 1st I thot it was, a come down fr
the heavy of pleasure-measure; but no: obviously you pronounce
"leisure" the same.

It is, I think, that, a *negative* formulation is, in this last line,
required: to "rime" with last line of 1—the syntax has to be like backed
up.)

II.) but just as his head is long, his breath is quick & short, AND (which
is, of course, in a way, the same thing: any man who goes fast can't
go without, *etcs*, which are shorthand for the fastest sort of
juxtapositions:

>   it's JUXTAPOSITIONS, that I mean by
quick breath, and that you are not yet getting in [*added in margin:*
Etcs. *have to be got in*], at least in the verse: possibly exception THE
EPIC EXpands; certain exception, the LETTER (which I shall return
to you, but want back)

the negative of it: "The Primitives"—where the shortness comes
>   acropper (to me, that is)
(*the negative of (I):*"A Local Celebration"—which needs the

ANTIENT of "so temptings
green," the ARTIFICE, to
give the heart the fine
mind's wit)

THE POSITIVE IS, in these things, (ABSOLUTE) in the use of the
parentheses in THE EPIC EXPANDS—wow, they are wonderful, AND
ARE TO BE LEARNED FROM, by Creeley as well as by me, and
whoever else has got an ear to hear with: exs.:

 (or be
expanded by)
    (throw up)
      (will use)
        &, above all, *too (too)*

((figure, myself, you lose the care in (say): but all the others,
 especially (*he could not*
 stop there) or (*put back into*
 quiet)

   These things make the poem, and, if I were an editor, I'd
print it instantly for their reason, even tho I do not, I admit,
and I think this is yr fault, (tho one is willing, dealing with
you, to throw in my own stupidities (of a day)) understand exactly
what's going on:
    it is the three coke bottles
       (& the poets?)

that seem to be insufficient ambiguities, no?
      (Aw, shit, exkuse
the fingers, only, just becoz we're on the mat, here's two holes
this citizen finds)

ROUGHWINDS DOE SHAKE THE DARLING OF MY HEART is
confirmation of,
how antient is the heart of
Robert Creeley

(& if Ez wrote that gloss as of it, he
better go back to where he wants to go, in other words,
RAPA ROUND, N.J.)

(I do not like IRA)

Let me take this flyer (based, I suppose, somewhat as well on the
prose also enclosed):
         the reason why, at this juncture of time,
Creeley fights so hard for prose, is, that it enables him to get in, to go by,
that head of his, to let it play over, his things, outside objects (which
tend to be critical abstractions) is, BECAUSE HE HAS FOUGHT, AND
IS FIGHTING FOR, *CLARITIES On the Broad FRONT*—and is making
them!
         (and how!: witness sentence in front window this
letter)
         olson sez, "At same time, no reason at all, same Creeley
shouldn't be dishing up TIME & SOUND of that Creeley who has
personal torments"—the which, I figure, has to come boisting out in
verse, simply because verse is a TIME maker
         (note, please, cadence in
enclosed LETTER, especially in Creeley on his present living)

         IN OTHER WORDS, what Patchen, Miller ain't got (agreein
         with—and it is amazing how precisely I agree—passages
         excepted of Miller)
         what creeley's got, and can trust,

the slow, antient hart
         (what makes Leed, his friends, &
olson)

((say, do date yr letters at top: i lose envelopes, and then, where am I))
[*Added in ink:*] (Intermission one hr, clearing desk (one month or
more), finding yr letters & my mss, & ordering same: dreadful way of
reminding one self of time the bitch)

What I was looking for, was, yr prose. Will come to that. First

yr instinct, to have gone to Dunbar, & the curious thing, for me, I
took a crack at translating same into american some two months ago[93]

It is not my business (Dunbar: antients), but, given above premise abt
you, creeley, as true green, wassail, or whatever (the laughter, as you
read, the pertinence to see (impertinence) the ant, the centaur,[94] the
high ladye (o, let's all ride, love, the coach, the couch, it's May,
and, in the grand canyon, a rose petal, and here, where they dropped
annulets, I, am made a member of, the tribe—OH, the race has not
vanished, my sweet, it is only the sound of teeeth you hear, not
the racket of love-making: this, is to be found where the mound
(they built with plane's view, the long snake of a
cockerel's color, and we, we, who are no longer males, but sons,
SUNS are become our bizness, sister, and, if we leap on you without
intermission, that's the way it's gonna be, for a while, wile away
o green GREEN is the color of the[95] (ambiguous, sd mister Freud,
which sex is which, "and the riddle of femininity," and he thru up
his hands, and went off abt that Moses business,[96] which was more
right than he knew ANYHOW, creeley's
in there

THE FEAR OF DEATH CONFOUNDETH ME

And do you not like: "The sentence undulates, raising no song—it is too
old, the words of it are falling apart, only percussion continues,
with weakening emphasis, what was once cadenced melody full of
sweet breath."
                    Me, I think, that
                    can't be beat
                              And again I hear, our earlier masters: am I rite?
& "there never was another more another than this one"

Well, it's got god damned hot here the last three days, Washington is a
swamp
      and how i shall work the weeks ahead, who knows

                         One thing's
sure, I'll be in n.e. sometime soon.

                  and if I have a car, where is
Littleton? how far, from
Gloucester?

      But I'll probably not have a car (my friend in ny[97] is
selling same) SO:

           let language be our tie!
           And please write me what you
           think
                love,

                Olson

                          [Washington, D.C.]
                          fri. june 9   50

R. Cr.:

      the vulgarizations: too much (in the old sense)   the opiate,
for ex., of the ray-deo worse, much worse, than what historically
shrinking lenin talked his mouth off, about   ((do you know gorky's
days with lenin, AND his reminiscences of tolstoy? excellent, both))

a streetcar, which used to be (especially in Worcester when, they
were open, and made like French trains, and ran down freeways in back
of people's houses), or since, are now, here, with o people, the NEWS,
the latest, and mu-sick, mu-sick, mu-sick, worst than war, worse than
peace (both dead), and the people's faces like boils[98]

well, not the point   which is, to tell you how moved i am by yr plea
for the heart, for the return of, into the work of language:

i figure myself the *via* is from object, back in (for it has to be got back by
form (form, given yr definition only) not by the ways of the likes of
Mill. or Patch. (or EE, for the matter—nor do I mean Elderberry
Eggnog)
> rule #1: it is not to be talked about, to be descriptive of, or
> explode all over the place: that makes for the old pile of grease
> and shit, gurry, we calls it, where i hale [*sic*] from

I still believe the Path of Ezra is the 'oly won, even tho I do not believe
him capable of fronting to that which is thuggish abt the 'eart. (Is it not
true, that Ez [Ex?], is more fine than strong, that it is such gentilities as
rain, grass, birds on a wire, 5, now 3, Metechevsky or whatever, tents,[99]
the trillings, rather than the thrustings, that are where he scores? He
goes literary with lynxes, Dioces, and fuckings, and can only stalk thru
the heart-lands by the wit of attack, attack: attack on USURA, attack on,
by Artemis, PITY, cleanings, yes, but WE WANT SCOURINGS
                                                              where
the right is, is, that he goeth by language: this we must do, and do, and
do, otherwise we better go into, say, politics

Bill, good Doc, I think is now the more seen, because, from the
beginning, he has gone for his images to the running street of, to the
Passaic of (water poisoned with the dead   (cats win, in the urbe)   and
stained with dyes   (cats, & industry)   the brutal, but fruits, he has (has
he?) wanted beauty so hard
                              (AND WHO CAN BEAT LIFE INTO
FORM, who is
so foolish?

> (is it no only language, for the likes of
> uss?

If I were to put it another way—to expand upon the text, Beaute is
difficult, Mr. Yeats[100]—it would come to a matter (the heart would) of
syllables: measure our masters by 'em—

> miss moore merely mathematical
> mr cummings, quite vulgar (broad) abt 'em
> mr bill, getting 'em fr the scrupulousness of his attention to
>   the objects of which words are to him the nouns (he
>   is in this sense a beginner, gets back to, the *naming*
>   force/function of language (folk, city folk, his)
>
> Ez, i honestly believe (despite all his chatter abt
> mu-sick, & harmonics) does it (he does it grandly, as
> dante, sure) without thinkin' about 'em, does it, like
>   —In the drenched tent/ there is quiet
>   Sered eyes/ are at rest[101]
>
> does it, because, he has absolutely, single-mindedly
> (is that SINGLE INTELLIGENCE?) GONE BY LANGUAGE

((Let me throw in, for the gander of it, for yr lookins, and thinkins back,
   a sort of an arty piece done some time ago, and only recently stumbled
   on, for yr opinion: shall i, is it worth, bothering to publish? (the
   trouble with what was done (even yesterday) is, today, . . .) [*added by
   Olson in margin:* will look it over, 1st]

I think this whole matter of heart is, at root, content (again, in the
precision of yr FIRST PRINCIPLE: form is never . . .)

IS a matter of ploughing in, from the man, his content (& it better be
good) and forcing, always forcing on, not by way of it as statement, but
it as it brings abt its form, ONLY THUS, not

by the talkin of it, the posture of O LIFE, & O ME

                                             (REPELLENT,
ILL., or whatever city, state, the LOVERS come from, the tenement
boys, the O LET'S OBJECT, LET'S PLAY AND FUCK, THE LET'S BE
QUAKERS AND ANGELS ABOUT ALL THESE HORRORS
                                                              "o, let
us just believe in beyootie")

crist

(*note:* there must be, somewhere, a word/concept/putsch the extension
        of *claritas*   (better than olson's *"est hominis confusio"*)[102] for
        that
IS WHAT HAS TO BE ADDED

        sd R. Cr:
                   form is never more than an extension of content
                                          June, 1950

                                          amo

                                            o

_____
=======================
_____

                                          [Littleton, N.H.]
                                          Sunday/ june 11, 50

Dear O,
        Very grateful to you for the comments on the poems, etc. You do
me a great deal of compliment, that I doubt I merit, but good to have it,
anyhow. I think you hit the main things, certainly the main difficulties,
being the trouble with stretching the 'context,' making room, in the
poems: getting the whole in. You'll have the other poem at this point, I
expect. Useless to say much abt it/ just done (quick) and I cant judge it,
and let it sit. Here & there, in it, things that I do like:

that seems enough for the moment. Too, abt the prose, there you hit again: the whole push for that kind of writing, has come, in my case: from the 'freedom,' supposed or otherwise, that the frame gives. I have a liking for the play abt the thing, around & over: touching at angles. What they call, or have called: obliquity. It had seemed, or so to me, that there was no such thing as: a direct statement/ that much like the 'objectivity': this, as well, was a shorthand to: assumption of value/ justified or not. Like they say, that there is no straight line, it being close, that example, to the 'straight line' in prose (or poetry)—an excuse for hurrying thru. Beginning abt 3 yrs ago, I started with the stories, using that reasoning, i.e., the multiple 'plots,' or ways of looking, on the one thing, in which, because it cant be, no 'one' action is decisive. It began with (having a journal of sorts to work with) a tracing of what was put down there, as against: what I took as having 'happened.' That kept me going for quite a while. That is, the shading between the assumption of an 'event' and the multiple 'sensings' of 'value' in it: begin a very great deal. But fatuous, to talk of this. I.e., impossible that anything but the stories, cd show what was up, and all but a very few: are poor examples of the reasoning, because I cant, as yet, handle them. (Have sent two, in lieu of better things, the two I have the most liking for, being out at the moment, and I have no copies: L[eonardo's]N[ephew]: abt 3 yrs ago/ T[he]L[overs]: this past winter, being an attempt (exercise) to shake up the surface, and to get a better grip on mechanics: I send it/ only because it gives some idea of what goes on here/ tho, as usual, I've pushed a possible attitude, well beyond my own: call this/ Gide's Law.) Anyhow, it's work, and a great deal of it, like they say, to make the essentials of the craft/ to kick out the rot, and let the mind swing clear/ of the junk. What can I say here? It has been a kind of stripping/ that is: one begins with: pride in what talent he supposes himself to have/ one revokes that to become: humble in the face of his subject: one then grips the pride in that/ and what one does then: is his own biz. Possible 'stages.' Some having been my own. This gets me to yr note abt: who else is there. This, too, difficult to put down, or my own feelings abt it. That is: what, here, can I say—whom did you expect. Or what or when. Is there, dammit, is there: one other intelligence you wd grant other than you own/ I mean: to count on? Yes, delight, perhaps, pleasure/ & something to grind with yr own head. But that lacking/ or the talent/ proof:

lacking—how can it matter. I cant see that one writes/ or does anything/ to be one among others: but only to be: himself. The ONLY thing. He can be. There is, Olson, singularly, or otherwise: no one but yrself/ anywhere. There are: no examples/ no rules/ no precedents/ no staples/ no practisers/ that cd break in. To that cell. If you had been, & I expect you have: in a place where you are alone in this way/ certain things from books: wd have been, at times, very hard to read/ because they suggested a camaraderie/ or what you will/ that was a good ways from what you had: I mean here something like the bit in the Dr's American Grain/ the biz abt Paris: [103] I have read that with a good deal of envy/ even malice/ many times. It had seemed, now & again: that I should need that sort of thing. That being here, out of it, was my loss. When we first came, Slater had written me: you'll turn out another Yvor Winters, because it's the people, in NY, in such a place: that you should now be living with, talking with, & it is for old men: the country, or that kind of being away from things. Well, I move awkwardly in a city, painfully, for many reasons: I had been brought up in the country, on a farm, and the language, the way I speak: is, or has to do with, that slowness & slow laps, say, around a center. That is: talk, god yes: for hours, days even: on one thing. Years, the same thing. When I did live in the city, the negroes were the only ones, believe me, that could talk that way. Keep on it/ and going. The feel of words. Among the ones/ supposed to be 'my kind' ('I am homesick after mine own kind' or something): who was there . . . The most helpless bunch imaginable, and only one or two: able to be straight: love, if you will: only one or two. And they as sick as I was/ and cut down by the place. We lived on the Cape for a time, but that was hopeless. We had got ourselves a good rent, for the winter in a summer cottage/ we sat there all one winter, by ourselves (and it WASNT being by ourselves that we wanted, certainly), the baby was born: I remember going up to a woman's house, she having called: abt 6 words abt the baby: 4 hrs on the impossibilities of Marxism. It didn't seem it. So, we bought the place up here. Here we are. Two & a half years now. The people: farmers & lumbermen. Someone to talk to. A few nights ago: we took the truck over thru Bethlehem & down the back hill into Franconia. Coming down, you come to old fields, cut out of the woods, that have been left. You can look out, across the valley, at the

mountains. I mean: it's bed rock, with that around you. Say: 48 hrs of
the week it wont be, but it's still there: to get to. Last year/ was coming
up thru the notch with one of the neighbors, and the car broke down: it
was at night/ and these mountains, all around us. There were three of
us, and the man's kid. And he was ready: to walk over the mountains:
14 miles: home, carrying the kid. I talked him out of it, but, dammit,
he could have done it. He can make his way thru these woods, in any
weather, night or day: say, 6 generations (Ainsworths) all within a 50
mile radius: of this spot. Someday: you'll have to go thru the woods,
with that man: a new world. Anyhow, that wd be it/ we speak of an
'art': it is that kind of being there/ and able. In 1870 on: say: my
mother's family was living at Head Of The Tide: in Maine: you'll
remember as having made E. A. Robinson. My grandfather used to go
out on those ships/ 2 & 3 yrs at a time. Transplanted to Mass/ later/ my
grandmother was the same woman: with 9 children. When she was abt
20 or so, she had made the tour West: with Wendell Phillips/ met Mark
Twain, etc.[104] But married poorer, than even she was to begin with:
which was a poor relation. My other grandfather: was a farmer who
lived in Mass/ 6'3'' . . . & what this has to do with it, I dont know. My
grandmother knew a good many of the songs, would sing them. Her
father used to fight Indians/ it goes back into: what doesn't matter,
now. But we look for roots, and as with families, some of them: so
with these things, too. Now & again: someone like yrself: can make
me believe that, even at hand, right now, things are happening. Most
of the time: slush, slosh, shit. But to get back: 'tell me abt somebody
. . .' I wouldn't know one/ other than Bud [Berlin], and he hasn't
begun yet; other than Leed/ who's afield at the moment.

Abt the older, or the Cole group (in the Celebration, which I haven't
seen): you will know that Dostoyevsky, is a good deal closer, to us, or
to anyone, for that matter. Or Melville. There is no reason: not to
make use of the closeness, to make it a line. Of course, for me, all of
these people, are the poems, or the vague names. Many times I've tried
to see, like they say, what EP wd be like, talking, etc., what sort of
face, man, being. I get back to the work. What else. The same with the
Dr, with them all. (Selfishly, I am the only one: who is alive . . .).

Wd like to see the story, granted you have the time. Have seen very little prose that I can take to, in any way. That is, being written now. Well, so much for that. When you will.

Tell me when you will be around Boston & Gloucester/ am going down sometime soon, myself, and cd make it when you might be there. Wd be good to see you. Let me know.

All best to you,
Creeley

A note abt a letter from P/ today: and each time I put these things down: I feel like Aaron Burr/ ETC. So keep it cool/ or yr lad is DEAD. Eh?

This: 'Believe Olson FUNDAMENTALLY (not superficially) wrong. tendency which will sterilize anything it touches. i.e., AGAINST nature's increase. But Cr/ must judge for himself. shall try not to return to the subject. Merely telling Creel to WATCH the effect of certain bottom ideas; wot comes FROM certain seed. . .'

Now: what the fuck is with you & the old man??? This is: stupid. I mean: it's only/ dig. I had answered (going as far as my intuition cd reach, which is: short: these days): 'acquisition. . .' wd be against nature's increase/ in the sense that it wanted to make 'different' what was, etc. BUT cd also be for/ as one wd want to partake of/ in order to be in. That is: a container can take the shape: of the contained: which remains: center. . . We had spoken of this. I dont think that's what he kicks abt/ (I dont know, god knows) . . . I sd: if a man wanted to make himself/ for HIMself: that wd be one thing/ but to make himself/ the nature by way of the outline: that is another & is AGAINST no nature. Nature IS constant, etc. No: what I did say, tho some of the above, as well: 'O's belief in this: 'Form is never more than an extension of content. . . .'/ how cd that get to: 'AGAINST nature's increase. . .'?

You will know abt these things/ I, I feel it matters little.

June 12

I had a copy of M[*ontevallo*] R[*eview*] from DP (Sat/) and then today yr own letter (2nd) & one from Vince in Gloucester. (Somewhat sad: he had written this fine thing/ to have to acknowledge 'later': that he'd got the poems back/ this is the bad part of the biz. . .)

Well: yr poem there in MR is fine/ is good.[105] I like a little of one or two of the others (or more sound in them): but this has the head & the depth. I cant make (here, for example) the 'wrong' direction. [*Added in margin:* or how P gets that way—] Obviously: this is the translation of a spite? Tell me. Annoying to sit here/ with none of the pieces. A curse, etc.

Also this: from a letter from Emerson/[106] re yr poem & bk:

'Olson sent me a longish poem & a copy of Y&X a week or so ago. I've only had time to look quickly thru both, but the booklet looks sound, and the poem likewise. My sincere thanks for your putting him on to us. . .'

Also this note from Seymour Lawrence, editor of WAKE (up, you shits. . .) but I had gone, like they say, to school with him: was one of the ed/ of same: when it was at Har/ also with him. (He bugs me, but): '(at last) . . . Read a poem by Charles Olson in IMAGI, and I liked it; anxious to see more of his work. . .' What cd you send him, say: cd: I expect, give him what we have (but I hate to) & hope you dont drop dead. Say what you think. His address: WAKE Editions/ 18 East 198th Street, NYC. The thing there: they got a nice circulation: being handled by Jose/ Villa: one shrewd apple. He was making up: the issue for Sept/ so better get it there, if you have it: or let me know abt what we have. Have written/ asking if he has, still, room.

MR: real bad/ all in all. (A letter (short(from Payne: what's his kick???) [*Added:* Saw thing in NINE.[107]]

Dear O,

A note on these 2: Leo's Nephew, was written abt 2 summers ago. I.e., up till that point, had let the prose sit, and this was, I think, the 3rd or so, of a series written that summer, when Leed was here with us. The point was then: to make obliquity a valid technique (not that I had that in mind, GOOD LORD, but that's what it came out as: this was abt the 3rd best, or the one of several I kept over; Accent having, still, the best: being: UNGRATEFUL JOSIE & RICHARD THE LION (a story well calculated to keep you in: SUSPENSE. . .). No: I digress. Anyhow, shall we say, the leaves colored & fell, winter came: we sat. In my chair, me & in her chair: her. Yes. (& the boy) Yes. Well: that fall, had written a long-winded thing abt the city, & then that spring: a series of things abt: what happens when nothing happens, etc. That summer, mostly poetry, but some prose, tho I cant think of any, offhand. That is, the spring: THE UNSUCCESSFUL HUSBAND (which is what KENYON will print: someday). Also: 3 Fate Tales/ which was the right slant (being equal digressions round a 'theme.') Well, up to last fall: when I took it as to the point: to loosen up/ the sound, & method: to make room for/ the unexpected, etc. (a novel dropped on the way: I cant write that, or them, NOW, tho always wise to say you are writing a novel: to accn't for lack of goods). No: but it came to: taking seriously, shifts in possible action, focus, surroundings, speech, getting A in & OUT of the room, etc., etc. Mechanics. Of which the 2nd story (Lover) is an instance. [*Added: practise*] (And a laugh. . . i.e., I sd note, ACCENT'S comment: 'Like so many of your stories that we've seen, this one has a good deal that we like, yet the over-all effect is not completely favorable. Your style, which gives the piece much of its interest (HO HO), seems at times to be too personal (I'LL SLAP YR FACE. . .). You seem to be "in" your story too much (HEY JOE: GIVE ME A HAND WITH THIS. . .). I think that what I'm trying to say (YR TRYING, GOD KNOWS. . .) is (IS) that we felt (I FEEL THAT WE SHOULD. . .) that this story generally (*AND*, DAMN YOU, *AND*: SPECIFICALLY!!!) lacked control (LOOK   O U T . . .). I realize (I know, I believe, I

think, &: I am of the opinion. . .), of course (of course), that this is
(IS) part of the story's charm (charmant) (n'est pas. . .[*added:* who?] is
that 'right': sp?), but (back to work) there must be (should be, at least)
a happy medium (and so: undso, we leave (gang aus) aus, aus,
the. . .   people? NO.) . . . . . Sorry to hear about your trouble with
the chickens (but I must make it clear to you that we are unable to
concern ourselves with the rigors of yr domestic procedure AT THIS
TIME. . .). . .'

(t o m   t o m)

phew.

Well, THAT story. I think the sooner we leave out the 155 million
people who MIGHT read any given work, etc., and get back to who
WILL: namely, yrself, etc.: the cooler/ things will be/ all round. I
enjoy it. I like it fine.

Creeley

(that's too much: yr style seems to be too personal: ha
 that's too much: yr style seems to be too personal: ha
 that's too much: yr style seems to be too personal: ha
 that's too much: yr style seems to be too personal: ha
 that's too much: yr style seems to be too personal: ha
 that's too much: yr style seems to be too personal: ha

[Littleton, N.H.
14 June 1950]

OK

what's next

[*A typed note, with Olson's remarks in the margin:* 6 / 14 / 50
enclosing *Littleton, NH,* (interesting, maybe more so than, S[later]
B[rown],[108] but not so close as SB)]

[Littleton, N.H.]
15/6/50

Dear O/

Tell me how these things sound to you, when you can get to them.
Impossible for me to judge/ flux & shakeup: that they are. Which is
good. You have done that much: my thanks.

Have a cold/ still: headache & heat is a bug. My 'condition.' Fuck
that. Well, what's up. Like they say. Write when you can: very tough
hanging these days.

Best/

[*unsigned*]

'Doesn't it seem strange to you, Marie, that in this modern day . . .'

[*Note by Olson at top of letter:* enclosing Slater Brown—Hart poem]

[Littleton, N.H.]
june 16/ 50

Dear O,

Had been thinking, after the poem to Slater, of HC, and then
went back to the poems. Too much/ those things. I mean: of the heart,
that which can be tracked—how? By feel. It is the way there; I cant
think of another. Incidental to this, yr comment of EP's going by feel/
GONE BY LANGUAGE, you had it. It is the difference, between him
& Eliot/ always was. The last wd plot the 'heart,' like one wd nail a
butterfly to a board/ no different. Inescapable: we have it/ or we dont. It
is that coloring, to our possible words: we cannot manufacture.
Reading much that has been written in the last few years (as one wd
naturally look for 'associates'), have been struck, even down, by the
mechanical quality of the verse. You will remember, perhaps, the loud
touting of Shapiro's ELEGY FOR A DEAD SOLDIER (or
something).¹⁰⁹ Not, here, to be snide/ but it is a pathetic thing: where
LOVE cd lift, beyond & into: this flops/ on the 'facts.' What can it be
more/ the 'transformation': but that color & shape. Well. To go back to
EP/ the early stuff (PERSONAE, etc.): was it luck, then, that pushed
him to the Provencal, to Kung, etc. Was it not: only these: were love
articulated. Stammerings (these are attractive, in that they make room
for the lesser of us): but clear, deep 'love': like Kung's/ admits no
fakers. Anyhow, thruout these (as oddly, with Stevens, too): (I 'feel')
that more than love of language/ there is the 'love' of what's abt/ that
the words: can bring into & over: the sensing. How can it be tracked,
then: that shape of the word round the thing/// or 'criticized. . .'

We know that it is a craft, that, like any tool, instrument, the
particular uses of it, must be learned. The ways. That, for example,
ineptness, the clumsy touch, can so blunt & disfigure the sensing/ that
it's impossible to take it in.

(Raining: Dave, our boy, exclaiming: JESUS, JESUS: WATER!)

Here, he had shown the shortest way/ to mark, by ear & close looking,

what had been put down: before. He had it: the Eliz/ lyricists, the
finest sounds, in any tongue: to tune in: to that. Method: you had said
that. It is what he has: but deeper. We work, say 4 hrs/ 48 hrs: a week:
to arrive at: 'to contain,' 'to be contained.' I have been arguing,
elsewhere, with a man who takes it/ there is pedantry there (and there
is), who cannot get rid of his own 'sneer,' to cut straight thru: to dead
center, to the wonder of these things. What Pound can be: is a poet/
and damn few are. Well, weak/ that. To mean: here & there, among us/
the speech, beyond the 'facts' & nothing else can make:
reality.

   What had so cursed us/ as to make these exclamations:
'reasonable' . . . Dont be emotional. Control yrself. Sentimental. Yr
feelings are excessive. Enthusiasm. Childish. I dont want to talk abt it.
Now be reasonable. Keep yr head. No use getting excited.

                 I mean:
insofar as: a direct reaction from the THING, was blocked by such shit,
we began to fumble, & slop/ sophistries. True: how cd an 'emotion' be
BUT excessive when the least tear: is suspect. A long time ago: I had
read that in Italy, men sing in the streets. I cant forget that. Too, there
are countries where men can cry. Nor that either. I want to move
there, some of these days. (Like they say: is there anything more
pathetic: than a MAN crying. . .) What is the matter with them/ these
people. Men/ as women/ as children: should be ABLE to be moved/ to
cry. . . One of those awkward times when I found myself crying in a
public restaurant/ and escaped: just in time. . . Not tears in the soup:
what am I saying. . . BUT: I know what you MEAN.

   Well/ here we are. You: spread the feel & grip of the
content/ like & in keeping with: content. Closer, one wd like to see: the
push that makes such things/ that sounds out, deep, in things like
MOVE OVER &, strange, that where you say, 'document means that
there are no flowers. . .':[110] THEY ARE BLOOMING. I mean: The
Burning Babe, etc. To cut to a language/ with color, & dimension,
beyond its 'sense': that's the job, or so I take it.

You know: that Hart Crane used to go by feel, and what else. I mean:
as Slater talked abt him, he was the one I'd put the money on. He used
to: say the poems/ conversation, before he wrote them. Many times/

they wd be talking, and the words wd simply be there. Like: BACARDI SPREADS THE EAGLE'S WINGS/[111] just such an instance. Then/ 'composition by field'/ with him: out of the Thesaurus/ he was looking for (NOT SENSE) but the sound, color, and WORD: that cd make the (basic) sense. By feel. Slater had told me, that he & HC, started to learn Spanish together. And abt that time the Prez of Mexico had come out against the Catholics, which excited Crane, much, so he decided to write a letter to the Prez congratulating him on his 'stand.' And began it (how else): Caro Presidente. . . And cdn't see: what was wrong. Well, what cd be, with such a man. I mean: one word/ there was never more than the ONE word. Coupled in him, as S/ had it: the literal, & (impossible): the Crane/ what he cd feel/see/find : in any word. When living in an apt/ house: Slater sd, he went to see him one morning/ and an old tree by the house, stripped of leaves, etc., was dripping: typewriter ribbon, and going up, he heard shouting coming from C/'s room: and went in: to find the landlady & HC/ locked on the floor, fighting: over the typewriter. And the landlady's shouts to B/ DONT LET HIM THROW IT OUT . . . AGAIN. Apparently, C/ had thrown it out the window/ six or seven times. And the landlady/ his gd friend/ knew that if he broke it:the game was up. He was, like they say, writing THE BRIDGE, abt that time. Tho the explanation for why he was throwing it out, was, it wdn't write Spanish. Things: real things: for HC. Everything/ came into him.

To get back: Tell me when you will be abt NE. Selfishly, wd like to get away from here, even for a bit, and wd, more, like to see you. If only for a short time. Things get tight, now & again, and some comment/ off & away from, the pressures, comes as relief, or cd. So say when you might be abt. Wd plan to come down, having a few other things to do there (Boston) as well. Well. when you can.

Best to you,

Creeley

[Littleton, N.H.]
june 17 [1950]

Dear O,

A difficult thing (you send me) to write abt.[112] To take it round the back way, etc. Where you come best: is where you center/ make around: a thing as tangible as THIS. I.e., we get here/ beauty . . . (& cd best say, perhaps,: is still (still) difficult, or: here, I find it hard to see by way of the document). [*Added in margin:* to mean: ONWARD, *with drawing of a charging figure carrying a flag.*] I dislike (I dont like at all) the going back to MOVE OVER and LA PREFACE, etc. BUT, but, we had the center of yrself there, most certainly. I cant get the corpus here/ the body or the heart/ more than what I am 'told' and I am a hard one, to believe. I/ here, that is 'I' is NOT the eye in MOVE over, the looker/ who sees with force, but is, instead, rambler. That is, the difficulty, as a reader wd judge it, of yr style, is to maintain a logos, a power of method, derived from (form) (from content)/ that lays bare: yr center, or: of what use the document, IF: no final stripping, can be effected. You say that yrself/ to yrself. I serve no function here.

But this is hard on what's good there, and much of that, tho: I miss the tightness of the others, & the sweep. What had pushed you in IN COLD HELL, etc., what has to push you, if you can be pushed, and you can, etc. (The 1st 2 lines of 3, I like.) Also of II/ but too close to: the surface/ glances: off. Where it should: dig in.

Well, fuck it. You do better. Impossible to like them all, or it would be possible. Always: the way, certainly.

Best, that you tell me what you think of this/ or if: you take it makes it.

Bitter & useless work/ that this is. (For what: for whom: why.)

Again: let me know when you'll be abt NE. Wd much rather talk, then.

Let me see the story, when you can get to it. Lousy day: rain & still the cold. Am in no MOOD to confront the problem of beauty/ you didn't break me down. Stubborn, etc. Mules.

Will write again soon.

(get even) comment on the last two sent you, when you can. Also: if you think the prose, hits anything.

(i dunno)

Yr lad/
Creeley

YR MOVE, MR OLSON

Later: let me put it another way/ like they say.

(Day/
           diminutive . . .) you dig?

I mean:
(Well, still, is there anything . . .)
(but this is (this bone) still (still) no reason)

I mean: truly, those are gt/ words. All three: sets.

Well, we will get there (you will) (I will) & why not.

[*Added at top of letter by Creeley:*]
I wanna be GOOFED but only by pot.

C. Parker, looking at a photograph of himself at the age of 6: 'I
          was a clean little bird then . . .'

when yez be in NE???

[Littleton, N.H.]
june 18/ 50

Dear O,

Just a note abt a letter here today from one of the editors of MOOD (a damn sad little affair, but cd be as good as any, granted somebody takes hold there).[113] Anyhow, they had sent me on a copy of their EP no/ and had written them: you are all over the place. I.e., notes/ concise/ listing of sources: etc., etc. OUTLINE. Can get to, in short space, the basic/ ways in: to subject: Ez. So they write back that they are going to try again in their Sept/ no: and ask me to do what I had said should be done with Pl's work (poetry & craft, economics etc.) Well, I am not the lad/ tho I wd like to see it there, nonetheless. I had remembered yr listing of the fundamentals in a letter to me/ that WAS it. So, wd you [be] agreeable to helping them out on the head of 'poetry & craft'/ the way you had it there/ tho even a barer outline: wd stick just as tight. Then, too, I take it, it would help to point to three or four basick sources for getting in to the stuff/ and the head that was putting it down: comment like some of that in MAKE IT NEW, etc. I sd think it cd run abt 2-4 pp/ but I wd take it: the briefer/ the better.

You see what this issue cd be: a basick handbk, for the logos & method: of Ez. Is that needed? YOUR MOVE. O well. Are they pushing you these days? I mean: cd you get to something like that. A note as soon as you can wd be a help/ so I can tell them/ what might be available. If you write it/ it'll go in. Count on that. Make it right on the ground (we lost). They print in August/ so when you can: but send me word/ if you are willing/ as soon as you can? Yes.

All best to you,

Creeley

Odd, that today I had a letter from Slater, after some time. And says he will be coming up here, if he can, some time next month. Hows that for dreams, eh?

Well, he is of the best.

He is sitting by himself in Patterson/ NY. Reading. Too much. Jacob

Boehme. As he says/ stuff I sd have read before I was thirty/ he is now reading. And back to it: the work: this winter. There is one/ cd (and will yet) write some gt/ thing.

Well, re this: let me know when you will be in NE/ (this gets to be whining): but want very much to see you/ so say. I.e., S: coming in July, and wd like to know when I might be going down to see you/ in B, or environs. So: say, when you can figure it.

On the goats/ S: 'I should like to see N.H. again and to see all of your family and most particularly the goats for I am very fond of them, though not for the reason given in the old Turkish proverb that you may know—Women for necessity, Boys for pleasure, but Goats for delight . . .'

O well/ when you can.

Will be looking.

[Washington, D.C.]
mon.   june 19   50

rob't: why   the old son of a bitch   Look: the enclosed is going to him the moment you send it back to me (I want you to see it 1st, just so you know how cool I am, and so, the record is,
full)
        I agree, it's
amusin, (I almost sd, hey, Peg!)

                        By JEEzus: it MUST be, that
he and DP (dirty p) ((she's
the poison in the soup))
                        —for let us remember, the 1st swing

at Olson, was BEFORE he had seen the verse, was going on,
the trouble these days, hersay, BEFORE you sent him pomes &
letter (the Goodman join)

              In OTHER WORDS, it just must be that,
the two of 'em ((you will remember letter to you on me as
semite and whirld saviour))
fell into my trap: otherwise, why
the seed (what is, in the DOCTRINE,
contra naturam?), who am I but, BUT
a fellows jew?

        u-sure-are

        wrong, ez

        OLD G (for
        generation)

                love, and more to
                come (been balled
                up, with—

                      wot is that
                attacks the balls?)

                  olson

[*Enclosed letter to Ezra Pound:*]

Look you old bastard if you want open war come on it and get it. Only
fercrissake stop this goddame sly dirty old sneak trick stuff you're
spreading around.

God damn you,
come in straight. That's my question. Can you?

Either put it up the way you're putting it up
full exegesis, straight on, to whoever

Or shut up.

Stop the filthy hints, where you don't know
the facts. Or decide, wot you are

Fish

or cut bait, Old Man:

so now it's below the belt stuff,
and I can't jibe it with (Spencer, dead, whom I might have
wished so), to whom EP sd, he
saved my life[114]

(thank you, old buck)

So now wot's yr

bug up yr ass?

(Even those whome you strike out at me to,
ask)

Olson

[Littleton, N.H.]
abt the 20th o' june, i wd say [1950]

Dear O,

Here's some conjecture/ what abt the tie-in: Hart Crane with
Melville. I mean: language & beat: & head/ similar (if we are listening
below the words). Much the same with these two. Reading Crane these
days.

What had come between, say, us (here) and him. Who is/was:
eloquent. Is is/ it [*sic*] that we are embarrassed/ as the Dr has also been
cause for same/ in some cases/ with some.

To learn: one can learn a good bit from HC/ that I cant see
he can pick up elsewhere. I.e., in Ez & the Doc/ Stevens (those noted
before) we have not this: pushing way out/ that is in Crane. Who
begins: say, already well beyond most eyes. Reading: For The
Marriage Of Faustus & Helen/[115] as Slater had it: he cd read this stuff
like no man. I mean: the push there in the words/ came into the cast of
the voice.

So much for that. (Only: that he seems oddly out of it/
for so many, at a time when he is of very apparent use, from many
angles. It is also odd/ our reactions/ to one of 'us' who does jump. (Like
a trick he had played.

What is it like in Wash/ these hot days. Must be/ bad. Here, almost
below freezing for the last two nights. Great fear: that the stuff planted
wd freeze, etc. That of it, which was up.

Wish that I were, at this moment, pushing out for someplace new.
During the war, with the ambulance, many times: half/asleep: wd be
supposing I was carrying the gd/ word from Aix to Ghent, or some
such. Pounding/ down the roads: at abt 3 miles per. What a mess/ the
Sikhs, per exemplum, begin to 'prepare' to meet the Maker/ as soon as
they get a scratch. This: a long involuted wail/ shaping itself over a

range of abt 6 octaves. Never/ stopping. So you can see what it was, say, with abt 8 of said S/ all with this one gig: I was out of my head those days: with or without stimulus.

I mean: hot. Too much. When in Mandalay/ after it had gone down: 130 in the shade. We climbed up the Pagoda there. To stagger all those steps/ to get to three rotting bozos on the top. Just enough left: to stumble down again. But some of those places: the living end, like they say. I mean: those big Pag/ you go into: little cities/ all kinds of things going on in these little passages/ all dark: with oil lamps, say, people shouting & having a great ole time. Then smack in the middle: a big statue: going up, to the top/ some 50 to 75 ft/ high: tall/ BUDDHA. You cd get the logos: with all this life round his feet. Kids & goats & everybody/ everybody: was there.

Take, for the subtle 'way': had tea with one sport/ and what it was: he wd pass me a little dish of varying herbs, etc. which I wd put a little of/ in my mouth: one thing at a time/ the POINT: the shiftings of taste/ like color: on the tongue. Then/ quietly spit it out. That was the point too. Just this little/ stimulus to the palate. Cdn't we live like that (with some wistfulness.).

O well/ when you can: write/ & say
what's up.

Best/

Creeley

[*Added at top of letter:*]
#enclose a fragment: for fun/ & when you have done: (1) eat it or (2) burn it. (the enemy......

[*Handwritten by magazine editor on top of printed slip:*]
Thank you for your trouble.
The editor.

The editor of "VARIEGATION" wishes to thank you for submitting the enclosed material and regrets that he is unable to use it. Your interest and accomplishment are appreciated; you are helping in the creation of a whole new world of free verse voices.

[*Added by Creeley:*] Me what whoosis?

o really   no trouble at all

                                                    [Washington, D.C.]
                                                    tuesday   june 20   50

hey dere, R. Cr.!

            Yr boyz have come in, and how, S. Lawrence
yestiddy, Dick Emerson tiddy:

                        Emerson goes up on Preface, Kingf,
and Cold Hell; and makes this proposition: that I give him some
shorter pieces like the others in *y & x* for his next no., GG #1, Series
3, the fall, that he hold CH for an anthology of O in either #2 or #3
(which same, with already published things such as Kingf, be then
offprinted as an O Chapbook of 150-200 copies)

                                            An all-out,
attractive proposition, is it not, and I will accept, but only after I have
heard back from you, for I'm yr boy, as you gather, and though I don't
expect to drop dead (despite the present strain), I should want you to
measure (so far as you can) what yours and Leed's publishing plans in

the same calendar as this of Emerson's might come to (so far, that is, as olson's work is concerned)

My own impression is, that this Emerson deal amounts to a gathering up of what is *now done* (the Chapbook a sort of 2nd *y & x*), and that what you and I have going, is strong enough to be, both between us, and vis-a-vis yr MAG (yr Burning Babe [*added:* or whatever; has it yet a tentative name?]), a projective, day-smashing, on-on business, open and alive, with the work between us taking on, from each other

(it is curious, how work done is, dead, and how possible work, scaring the shit out of one, is still the only alive thing, the only attraction)

You say.

Also, will you help me on WAKE? I looked over stuff yesterday, and (by the same above principle) the only stuff I wanted to send, is that which has been directly done, (1) what you already have, ADAMO, and (2) THE STORY. I am reworking a couple of unsatisfactory spots in A, and propose now to make final copy of STORY, to send to you. Would you give both yr good eye, and, if you think they're it (knowing WAKE and Lawrence), either ship them, or, what is probably better, tell me to? If not, I'll make up shorter pieces, but, at the moment, I should like to throw out into print these longer things, believing in the problem of form by such content,—and pleased as hell that, in this instance, one can get print before two months are out

(You will know the goddamn drag, by which we go, one year after we have done a thing: ex., Cold Hell will now not show until what, next spring? Shit)

This is a note / business

olson

[Added in ink:]
(1) 1st report: in the flush of final copy (*Adamo*)
    I am taking it on, myself, & sending A direct
    to SL—& to you the carbon, for any action/reaction
    you choose   (It's a pisser, thicker than anything yet. Only,
                    I don't think it's opaque. Hope not. ((There's
                    water, if not light!))

                                        AND (2)

ditto, on STORY, carbon enclosed — I plunge,
& send 1st copy to S.L.,
with less afflatus than of A,
but, there you are, verse ....
and more on the wife's go-by than
my own

                    (hope these don't put you
                    on yr face in those
                        quarters, friend!

P.S.
And look—as of P for Pisspot,
I don't see any need, now that I have had my spit,
by sending it to *you*, yesterday, to post
it also to him, if, for any reason, it
would serve to HANG you, there,
with the Master

[Littleton, N.H.]
June 21—50

Dear O,

If I keep hitting the biz re seeing you, forgive—not to suggest an
expiration of hopes elsewhere, simply that it now seems important to
have that chance to get to some of the things suggested by the letters,
tho impossible that they should get the full weight there. I mean no
more than: who is around these days, somewhat in the sense you had
it, in a recent letter, but more: who is around that can come over, thru,
for me, for those like Leed et al. Fighting with the writer of the notes,
the indicter of these presents/ as he had it: abt yr own groundsense: I
am crippled by no little dogma & inexperience. I know: I am right/ but
that matters little. Nor is he, less right/ for his purposes. But it is not
NOW that he is dealing with/ nor what's to be coming. In some sense/
let us now deride the smugness of Pound's followers: I have thought
that often; at the beginning, had written such a note to H[orton]/ to
forget to mail it, and then to get into the correspondence with him, etc.
Well/ out of it, it is. In many ways: foolish that I am in this, any of it,
since here I am, alone, and here I damn well mean to stay. A yoking up
with divers & sundry is an effort, hard to consider, tho nothing to do
with the big cheese possible, etc. : simply, my own nose, is all I can
follow. God forbid that it should be pinched by their fingers, etc. To
talk, then, not abt art, which is a topic not for a man with full
possession of his senses/ but better: simply, again, the drift possible,
what gets to ground in spite of itself, any afternoon, anywhere. Or
should. Because/ much talk from the others: but from yrself: the facts
of the poems/ the prose on P/ & the verse. The letters. That wd be
enough, any one of them. Having eyes, etc., was able to SEE what you
can do. I dont see it being done in any sense, kind or condition/
elsewhere. Simple enough to flatter anyone: but very difficult to make
plain wherein the basis for a trust: puts itself. I wd take as the
first obvious & most 'clear' step/ in making a way for oneself: to
make 'there' oneself: the tempering of method. Or, simply, the
acquisition of one. Insofar as anyone IS derivative of a style current,
rather than its USER, he is, briefly, damned. But as before/ content

being the shaper: it is, too, that looking for the content/ its root: in the head & self: that takes the time. ('Why do I write today . . .') Well, a time give to that, most probably, a long time. 20 yrs? Or something. A long time. If one is striking off, for oneself, free of the 'existing' forms, then the product is presented with an apparent 'quickness' (Stein, Pound, Williams, etc.). But just as we go thru the whole of Joyce looking for one IDEA, beyond the reiteration of echoes, & are somewhat put down, just so: an apparent logos in method/ new/ can mean no NEW content. A man, each man, is NEW. If his method, his form, IS the logic of his content: he cannot be but: NEW/ 'original.' But the changes, whatever, in an existing method, by a man coming up, will most certainly, not of necessity: mean: new content. In the sense that it must be. Lawrence was going by the head & heart. I had wondered: what kind of an answer to a question about his 'style' would one have got from him. . . I mean, what more than CONTENT? what more was the point. Less obvious, since he has been tagged so, is the 'stylist': Gide/ but why. . . That he had the strictness in his gripping of ways & means/ that he should make, for example, the 'neat distinctions' about conte & possible: novel. That a possible reader can 'see' surely, having been told, but much more to the point: that he see why it was again: CONTENT, that was pushing. Never a man worked more deliberately with his own vision/ seeing: than Gide. I simply cannot think of any that can pass him/ & so put him up with my own teachers: Stendhal, Do/, etc. The counterfeiters/ wd be enough to make the point. And the other work/ taken with this slant: then points the reason of its sometimes apparent slightness (I am thinking of the Isabel,[116] etc.) It is useless, altogether, to make assumptions about what can be done, until such a method is in the head. So, whereas a 100 idiots can flash in the pan, etc., yrself, one of the damn few concerned with a method/ that can get to the shape, be the shape, of yr content. Just there, for that reason, is my respect. Not knowing you, but for these letters, and they, much help tho they are, cannot make the point altogether. Well, that is why I should like to see you/ if & when you will be in NE. I wd confess/say/ I have to make a deliberate way of not being caught to or by: anyone, and that is no less fatuous than it sounds. Stupid, such a comment. No, I am here for the same reason anyone is here: to be so caught up. The sweet afflatus, or what you

had, something. The season.[117] It is. So when you can, give me word
on when you might be around. Wd not like to be obliged by other
things, and to not be, wd take some planning. So when you can.

Best to you,

Creeley

[Littleton, N.H.]
june 21/ 50
aft.

Dear O/
Had written you the other thing enclosed this morning/ and got yr
letter with the thing to P/ this noon. Let's pick up on that.

Hopeless for me to comment, more than what I know of you.
Knowing little, i.e., of what is the thing between you two, other than
what you have suggested. But TO BEGIN: good lord, what a fruitless
biz, it is. I mean: YOU/ why this stuff . . . you are putting it down,
straight: WHY get hung with this pettiness, in him/ DP/ or any of
them. We take that IN, god knows, OUR JOB; but to contribute: NO.
You are straight in the letter to him, but for what/ or end?

Well, I
am a yng man, like they say, & while Ez has the lift now, the ways &
means: we will outlive him. That is our function, to go beyond, in
time, in reach, in the head & heart. Many times, in the past few weeks,
for my own mental well-being, as the Dr had it: I've had to throw what
I cd at him/ AGAINST this bigotry & pettiness/ as the little periodicals
he has sent: push it. And this morning/ somewhat along the lines of
the letter written you: I was holding to you, as against him, as I have
often these past weeks. But to get to it, again: who is but you/ say: I
mean, where it counts/ or Ez: those are now echoes/ & vague shapes:

those. I mean: the sharpness & the use is IN/ side. What drags out, pulls into useless & stupid quibbling, is a drag on the energy that cannot be tolerated. CUT it out/ with what knives you can find. It is difficult for me, having lacked continually such a man to put it straight to, to realize what the current attitude may mean to you/ but IT EVEN DOUBTS ITSELF: (let me quote the part I had given: well I cant find the damn thing/ I mean, it was: querulous) When I had noted it for you/ had thought then: stupid, perhaps, to set up these ghosts for him. It was & is. I mean: how can you ACT on such drivel.

Sometimes, I think this ache/ this hate & damning of people/ is more than one is SUPPOSED to stomach/ and must cut out, go away: be alone. Like there are those: to be close to/ take them & to hell with the rest. Not this drain of useless attack & rebuttal/ on what IS NOT.

Well, old sport, you are not cool/ as we wd say. Not cool. Cool: is just that being able to ride such things/ that are not the point/ that do not cut into us/ as must the things that make us move. OR: one friend sits in a band in Boston 7 days a week/ what they call: a mickey band/ or pretty for the people. Useless to point to/ what it is or what he CAN make with his fingers & head/ there he is: to keep living. A contract for a yr/ and then more of the same. He looks to learn here & there/ and had told me that one bk he was reading on biology: had said/ 'Now go boldly buy a microscope . . .' I mean/ where are they: these others/ like even P/? But cool, that man is: he wd say, 'Please, let's NOT face it . . .' He is too much. OR Bud/ who will be setting up tourist cabins or some such/ in the Southwest/ to keep LIVING. ANYTHING TO KEEP LIVING/ GOING. And this sort of thing with P/ is BESIDE THE POINT. Or Leed in his deep freeze plant/ working for his ole man. I mean: cant we shake free of the commitment to answer, what NEEDS no answer?

Again, O, can it not be: that one sails/ out far enough/ to dodge such things/ or to steer clear of them? Not an excuse for being ABOVE 'criticism' but only that we should demand they make our reach, before they set in: to fight. I cannot take it Ez has the grip on yr way, he maintains, by the comment; or that he has, in truth, brought it to bear in the *against nature's increase* biz.

Pity, good crist, a good
bit of that: sd be headed to that place these days. Comments from DP
on who surrounds them/ what a nightmare of bilge that must be. I
think, often, of how he must be there: open to ALL COMERS/ almost.
That must be the end of it. Like she had noted the coming of one or
two/ whom she takes as : 'Important,' etc. But who to get back to the
push & the color & what COULD BE DONE. Who? More than the
fingering of little facts & NO HEADS to give them THEIR PLACE.
Well, shit, we have the strength & the push.

Why aim it at such as are
locked in?

His naming of those who cd be of help/ to you: I will say
straight: NOT ONE is capable of: HIMSELF/ I mean: to get to THAT
CENTER.

I sicken.

How can we continue, keep at it, lacking that renewal/ of what we can
give, and get, say. Lacking that kind of color to our living, etc. Well,
slush, to have it down that way. But it is what can sustain us. Most
certainly.

Read PG/ if nothing else comes to hand. I have seen him
there in his room with the wife kid/ (the joke): and at least know, cd
speak of this, & be understood. And dammit, I demand that. That we
not slide with the slush, that we go by the head & heart, FREE of the
slush, & slop. That we be there to TAKE whatever can be picked up &
thrown.

So/ quietly/ wd ask you, to hold the same way. What other way. Not
that I give that much, for my part in it, as go-between, ferret &
snooper/ which it seems. But that you keep clear yrself,.of what will
sap you/ uselessly, or why not go there yrself.

Christ: get there if
you can and see the land you once were proud to own, etc., or : shit.
Keep clear & go with & by yrself. Who is there/ that can make that
difference. I am ready, dammit, I am ready: to leave anywhere,
anything: at any time. You should keep yrself the same way.

Sadness & loss/ these: are useless shrines. Fuck em. Anyhow, why not go over there & see the old man/ and get to this: straight. Use names, say what's what: BE COOL. IF it means that to you. Tho no man's approval should.

            Well, fuck it. ½ sheer clouds & the other ½ : I wdn't know.

            But: say when you'll be about NE/ that's what I was thinking abt.

        Yr lad/

           Creeley

[*Added at top of letter:*]
Anyhow/ EP: hates people to be living *without* him.

         [Washington, D.C.]
         wed june 21 50

my dear creeley:

        1st, i have sent yr THE LOVER to Payne, thinking it the best yet, loving it (only want one sentence as "she" comes from the bath, to indicate, as has all previous uses of her, *her* response to *his* mood, why, other than nature, she rolls in against him)

                      I can't for the life of me, figure out that Payne has taste of any order, do not think he is a man of critique; he goes too fast, is an industry, does not gather, with his head, stays, for some lack of the simplest stems, sentimental. But I do not know many editors, in fact, he is the only one who is close to me, and it would give me deep pleasure if you, too, were to be one of the MR, whatever it is, just that we might be found together there. (I am still nervous abt it, but, in MR 2, at Payne's insistence, there will appear my only piece of prose outside ISHMAEL, a "story," i guess you'd call it (actually recollection—which is, I suppose, why I am nervous abt it), title STOCKING-CAP.)

2. Have this suggestion on the PROSE caper, if Payne sends it back (or has he, already, did you mean that, when you wrote you'd had a note from him? I've been out of touch with him since my return fr Ala.). Why not make it the follow-up to Olson on PRO VERSE, by offering it to Shapiro and Fjelde for the number after the coming one? They plan to use mine for a new rubric, Pick-A-Fight, or something. And maybe, then, I'd answer you, or something. Anyhow, I think that's one place for us to elbow our way along, beside the present rooms, cons[p]icuously yr MAG and this correspondence. What do you think?

(By the way, I'd knock that footnote out instantly, on PG, and Freud: if, given the annunciative form, one lets in present specifics, the annunciations suddenly all wilt.)

With the above in mind, let me go back over the piece, in returning it to you, & make scratches. (Done.)

3. Now to the verse, where, as ever, I feel on firmer ground (I mean, as far as olson goes). The one I go for, most, is SLATER'S. (I'm pulling this out to make a copy of, its "hart"; it comes out, I think, such a close, in, one.)

CREELEY, N.H.,[118] flares me, even more than SB, as you'd expect, knowing this Iranian (or do you? must, one day, ship you THE SHE-BEAR, and BIGMANS)[119]

> (and look here, R.CR. you mustn't be
> bothered by olson scratchings: it's the only
> way I can get IN, just as tho as it was my own,
> in order to come OUT, and say something to
> you? OK? Will henceforth, with this sd, and
> your understanding)

[*One or more pages possibly missing.*]

of a controlling constant, against which all the variations break and play.

What I did, with P[oor] S[eason], was to try to find that beat and flow, in order to point it up for you. I have a hunch, despite all the evidence of the 4 feminine, or 5, that, the 3, which characterizes that wonderful epigraph

> Are the mountains/ near the house?
> They are a force/. she said.

and the 1st line, so fine, which, to me, is still, on the
3 breath, (so:

> As thén, nów, indéfinite and poor

> ("and poor," that feminine
> "dying fall," of the mood
> *outside* us, conspicuously eliot's

> here, fine, following, the trochee
> feeling of the close-in 1st three
> feet)

that the 3, is very much a part of Creeley's "time"

> (Obviously, you, or I, as we read, wld read the epigraph,
> thus:

> Are the moúntains near the hoúse
> They are a fórce, she said

> I mean, that
we only bother to use the metronome when we can't discover the
musical phrase)

I'm not sure. Fast, I've just checked back over S B, and N H, where there is so much more of Creeley-time, and it looks (look at "Slater let me come home")—and opening of N.H.—that it is 3, which sounds base, dropping off to 2, coming on to 4, anyhow, worth investigating, just to get yrself, as you are.

Let's try it again, after there is more Creeley verse.

But it's absence (in the sense of its control) in P S is what stops me, here, where I am not stopped in S B, and N H. Or, clearly, in the prose, of the letters, or of THE LOVER.

****

Spent, must stop, now. And thanks, for letting me in. Please write me back just as soon as you can.

Yr olson.

Olson [*signed*]

PS: and, when you've had enough of 'em,
please send me back the carbons of, the
revised ADAMO, and of, THE STORY—have no copies of either.

[*In his letter of June 24 to come, Creeley refers to four letters received from Olson, not all of which have survived. The following version of one dated June 21, however, and another presumably from the next day, were preserved among Olson's papers, typed, with handwritten additions as noted. Their importance as the original form of the revised "Projective Verse" essay will be readily apparent.*]

[Washington, D.C.
21 June 1950]

The big baby, LINE—
                    it's the whole damned problem, in
COMPOSITION BY FIELD, this

keeping of the line PURE:

                              to undo free verse, its shittings,
we must hammer each line out as purely as each SYLLABLE,
or we're dead ducks, like

the Amygists,
or even EZ, when, as so often, in the Cantos, he
goes by his will, thinks
that it will carry him, he's
so strong. It don't, &
IT WON'T.

Let me start, putting it, this way: the syllable
is spontaneous, in this sense, that the EAR sez the syllable
[added in ink: (the ear, which has collected, which has "listened,"
around about] (the ear, which is so close to the MIND, (they are as
brother to sis), the mind the drying force

                        "poetry
                         is the dance of the in-
                         tellect
                         among the syllables"[120]

                                        half-right

It is incest, of which half the SINGLE INTELLIGENCE is born: fr the
mind and the ear, comes, sharp, the 1st of twins (always, Egyptians produced
twins, it seems)

             The other, the other child (together one has

SINGLE INTELLIGENCE—and a poem) is THE LINE, comes (I swear it) from the *breath*, fr the breathing of the man who writes. And only he can declare the line proper to him, its metric, and its point of ending—this

is where the work comes in, this is THE WORK, the beating out, the hammering (of which we die)

The trouble with most work, to my taking, since the breaking away from traditional and inherited lines, stanzas, and such wholes as Chaucer's TROILUS and MISTER SHAKE'S Lear, is

the characters have gone lazy *right here where the line is born.*

And I think, myself, it's softness of the brains, the crossing over, from where it belongs, as brother to sister ear, the philandering, of the mind, this screwing (it goes on in automobiles much more sensibly, the backseat) of the mind on the breath.

I have a hunch that, emotion being what it is, its control on our breathing is such, that any of us, who will stay out in the open, in the OPEN FIELD, will, unknown to ourselves

(was not this how line-form came into being in the 1st place—Sappho, or, the Canzone, say (behind them both

declare, every so often, unawares, a base beat and flow which will, order is such a part of the law of rhythm, also declare itself.

And I hunch, that, when a poem works, in the OPEN, it is just for this reason, of a controlling constant against which all variants break and play.

[The remaining section is handwritten.]
Adds, fr notes on Creeley mss.:

The annunciative announces itself, leaves *argument* where
it is, properly, in the preparation, in the self, BEFORE
language. *Observation*, likewise, belongs *previous* to act
of poem. Out, observation: cut to the energy, once you
have created the situation (context) to include the energy's
exemplum. And the *descriptive*, which, in verse, will
devil force.
[Creeley: has form (prose) only
           as it is such a going]

1 perception should lead *Directly* & *Immediately* to another
new perception

You cannot "engage" yr contemporaries: you either Kill 'em
                                              —or love him.

Tee-rew, tee-rew," sang the boid.

[as of a specific statement, too much so—or, in wrong place]
           It raises this question (generally), as of annunciative
           composition: is the Law, perhaps, this—that, when one is
           compelled to make a *statement*, one makes it flat, straight
           out, And does not mix (because of levitican businesses
           we are only beginning to explore) statement & image?

[Littleton, N.H.]
june 22/ [1950]

Dear O/
    Very good to have yr note abt Lawrence & Emerson. Had
suspected the latter wd make it, or so his letter had sounded. Very fine

gig. What you should be making. Will look most for that : single issue.
A spread is what you need/ to make yr own way felt. Well, both of
these gentlemen: to be straight with you—are a short or long way
(what matter): from my own sensing. Emerson: can be told/ and that
seems all that's to the point. When you deal with Lawrence, you are
dealing also with : Jose Garcia Villa. And that man is hopeless. But, to
look at the stuff with their eyes, for a moment (apart, altogether from
what it, in truth, is): 1/ it is 'experimental' (now a certain amount of
that has to go in each issue) 2/ it is 'new' (much that is 'experiment'
isn't, so that's a point in its favor) 3/ it has been published by several
'interesting' sources (Vou, Black Sun Press, etc.) 4/ it is written by a
man who is close to Ez (Jose is impressed by such things, and is,
himself, a friend of the 'gt/s'). 5/ he has written a book (this puts you in
with the publishers too, & is evidence of yr ability to make yr way in
related fields). 6/ he is someone to be 'introduced' as is Katherine
Hoskins (despite the interest in 'smaller' circles) 7/ he is in the
'approved' tradition (Williams, Pound, etc.) Well, quite bitterly, I wd
say you have little to worry about. Neither Jose or Seymour: know
that much abt poetry/ or the kind, particularly, I had been hitting in
these letters/ or you had, as well. I come to this: such, must be led by
the hand, & if one sees something he likes: push it/ to same. Now I had
been writing you well before I hit Emerson. Someone sent up a copy of
his CRISIS, a pamphlet dealing with current poetry, which was fair
enough.[121] So wrote him abt it. Then, when that poem of yrs (COLD
HELL, etc.) came by, it seemed the thing to push it on to him. Fair
enough. It takes little with a man like Emerson (tho his FIVE POETS,
is a lapse of sorts) to put him straight, re what is up, etc. This is NOT
egoism/ simply, dammit, that the fuzz is thick, & how to get thru/
clear. Any way seems fair. With Lawrence & the like/ anything goes. I
have called him an idiot many times, in my own oblique fashion, so no
need to worry abt what he may think of me. Etc. No, I tell you: it can
be done. Had done just that with KENYON on the stories, i.e., just
simply, gone thru in simple language, what was doing, there. It pays.
O well, this morning, now afternoon/ I am a little broken. As is Leed's
wrist he tells me, from an automobile accident. Well, wdn't you know
it, etc. Now what—I dont know, simply that that hangs us up for a
time. He says abt three to six weeks with the cast. And it may take a
time to get the use of it back. And, of course, all the printing hangs on
him. Well—a summer issue/ christ/ I'll do what I can. But am sickened

with slop & shit/ letters & the like, and think best perhaps, to forget/ & go back to myself. But will hang on. Re the poems of yrs we have. Wd like to hang on to them. BUT if Leed's agreeable, & you have nothing else there—cd, I expect, let you send on to Emerson the two shorter ones (tears . . .) well/ it's up to you. I'm too beat to take these things clearly in hand, at the moment. It seems like the works/ all hell: has broken loose. At the time/ when I had counted on moving.

Yr stuff enclosed. You had my note abt Adamo Me—the new draft reads better/ tho like others, still, more. The prose lacks the push of yr poetry/ or the sharpness. I like it, but it aint the end. Well, how much is, dammit. Couldn't say what they will think/ (they dont—so that's that). Just hold & see. Can make it sooner or later. Send on all you can to SL/ if you have more there. He's a hard man to please, because he doesn't know what he wants, to be frank.

Will shoot this stuff back to you, when I can go thru it more straight. They told me they were featuring Hoskins on this next whirl (Sept.) While I think of it: the way I had yr work lined was as follows. Morning News: this #1 at hand. (Supposedly: Summer issue/ say now: july or August. . .) Then the two shorter/ in #2. That is/the Fall No. Say abt Oct. We wanted to run these things off with not too much break in between. I have to see how Leed patches, to give you exact word.

Look sport: if it ever comes to yr own interests & ours/ Leed's & mine: yr own are it, obviously, & no need to mention other things. I cant say else. So whatever seems best for you, say it, and we'll make out.

I enclose a bit of doggerel/ these things for my OWN pleasure. Not really—but I am dead these days. This was just before the cloud burst. So it goes. Yr boy/

Creeley

[*Added at top of letter:*]
Did you ever try for a Guggenheim?
(Let's make that the next thing.)

Doggerel for O, Without ONE word changed, or even: corrected. [122]

Not so much time, as the head gripped round
itself and the inconstant, torn sound
of it pinned there, like a man, any man,
damned for five minutes under a ton of sand.
So it had happened, once, where the road
swings east along the ridge. The load
let go, and caught him. And his name.
Take it, whatever happens, we live the same.

But I was thinking this morning of things
I'd put down almost a year ago, things
not so much forgotten as out of it, or me,
hopeless to look at more, impossible to see
clearly. Such will be the usual, beyond
the irony and whatever I've found
is the use I've put it to. It was that way
came early to me. Useless to say
different. Anyhow, what's been done with
comes again this morning. To be able to live
with it—in the question that can hang
for days, years, in a song someone sang.

Looking thru books, I hit comment about
a man, by himself. So fair enough, to let it out.
He has it there: 'dull critter of enormous head . . .'
Allen Tate. And all I've read
of him could go in those five words.
God, could more of a man be less of birds
than that one (or the other rime could say it,
tho Willy Blake could damn the sullen wit
would turn on that, '. . . to shite
What might he not do if he sat down to write?')— [123]
Well, words & the sound of words that make
the sound of sense but cannot break
their dullness or the echoes of the head

plotting its dullness. I'd read
too much of it and Allen Tate was just the one
I hit on here. Useless to say, what he's done,
others do & did. But to forget, for a moment,
all this shit—let the sense find its element.

So much is useless that a head could trace
at fifty years its graces on the face,
by the lines there. Say that that crease
was twenty years with Joyce, the grease
that covered said crease, simply the sweat
that came of reading letters from Paquette.
I mean: how much time can you give to this
that can make you no more than its own foolishness,
or, dammit, I have time, god knows,
to stare at my hands or wiggle my toes
but tell me why I'm better off with Kafka
than with spending the same time with my own laughter.

Well, shit—this is a waste of time
of yours & mine, and the crime
is not so much this waste of effort
as it is that insistence that such will come to profit.
Because what the head can get to—
as we had it—is its image, what that would include,
and however they damn such egoism, to get to just that,
we have to strip down the verbiage, cut the fat.
And stare at what the hands are doing there
beyond Louis' 'enchantments of thin air . . .'
(I found that tucked away in Crane;
at the beginning of THE BRIDGE—the same
thing. Still, a man wrote me re Louis: you know
this young man is much influenced by Rimbaud.
Well, there again, the itch to pin down
and so cheapen, what a man may have found.)
To get back—the head & heart. An art
cd start there, or take that as part
of anything we'd try to make—

not Art for Art's sake.
But, again, the slogans can kill it.
It's not what we say but what we can will it
to be—to be there. In the sounds & what
they can grab to, words, the part
of us can come thru to ground.
The sense, the senses & the sound.
A little knowledge is a dangerous thing—and more
it makes a man a bore.
So we come home to Ez,
who lacks now only the fez
to make him the East. Or that man's way was sure
who said: I'd give it all up for Asia.
The graces of the Eastern mind,
shall we say, are marked by what it can find
about itself, & in, the natural.
We cant take that as all
but still it is that way that makes it new,
what it can, what it could do.

Leave it at this. At 24
one should be on his way to more
than conjecture or if we can yet see
the possible in impossibility—
I have somewhere to go.
What I can know
is what I can be.
And so I would be there with my own Don Quixote,
any evening, when the sun gets tired, goes down,
and ground is darkness and around
the mind the image is the darkness it can find.
Dammit, let's be led by the blind
like Cervantes that no world could make
a fool, or break
the laughter. Or, like they say,
get up (you might as well) with Rabelais.

Well, so much for this. Perhaps it comes to

just to see that I could do
it, sit down & push out this shit,
the sum & substance of it.

Anyhow, so much for rime.
It makes its time
dullness, & its beat
is irons on the feet
could run without it.
So it will sit,
where sounds will break
on it, hopeless to make
musick—
what is sick.

(They buried him near a dike,
so his friends can weep, as much as they like—

(They buried him near a city,
so there could be many to take pity—

(They buried him under the ground
to shut up forever his sullen sound.

(Later)
       sorry to sound so damn sour on the things you had sent. Reading
them over, with at least a tentative solution to the bugs re Leed's
accident, I can get away long enough to read them with some
'perspective.' Well, the story hits much better this second time thru/
well, let's be straight & call it a: proclamation/ it is. A good one. I wd
like very much to see it get in somewhere/ and why not WAKE. Shifts
& focus/ the self. In prose/ eventually/ the document will reach out, in
different ways from the (given) center/ must:to sustain itself, but here
is, certainly, the logos/ or the view: needed. And the weavings in &
out/ line lengths. They work there. The poem/ I am still not clear on/
meaning: here & there/ it's hard to grip the method, beyond its basick,
let's say that, logick. Perhaps I hang to the others, simply because this
is more 'difficult,' like they say, although, no, since La Preface & the

others/ the same depth. But as you had said/ what is MORE under hand: than what IS under hand. I have no eyes for else, re my own work; & even that is apt to bore. Or be, simply, not it. Which is worse. Well, the poem/ so much that I like there: the part abt building near water/ much of it. Simply: it dont hang together for me/ granted the logick/ as do some of the others. Well, again, I am with spleen at this point. Let me shake free & come back to it.

But do like the prose/ or that wedding, like they have it. It's a clear thing. What is up/ & around. Odd, I think of this, what is now common, perhaps . . . the biz of, say, waiting for the OFF beat to come in on a chorus. (And once Bird just sat thru the whole first measure/ or so: just waiting: for the right TIME) That's it.

[*Added at top of page:*]
Why not send S/L/ a copy of IN COLD HELL, if E doesn't object to its being printed previously; ie., that wd give him more to choose from.

[Washington, D.C.
22 June 1950]

[*Added in ink:*
breakfast butter:
excuse, please]

thursday —I'd call it, mornin', tho I dare say, for you, it wld be already half-day, but for me, who gets my licks in 1-9, to be up, now, as this rare day, at 9, mornin' time, is crazy: funny thing is, before 8, I came out of it, with the certainty I had dreamed a Creeley poem, both of you and by you but what, waking had taken away

it wasn't just that I had spent yesterday writing you abt the mss.—I
went on, last night, as I ate popcorn the wife had got up to make, 2 am
(we live crazy, coz she works a funny shift, 12:30-8:30, very pleasant,
long mornings, long evenings), to think abt the physiology of verse I
had blocked out to you yesterday, and abt yr fine letter on the prop., "I
am the only one: who is alive."

                                    No question, none. And you know
the sense in which I asked, "Who else is there": my lovely man,
Bolyai Farkas. For I have noticed, how true it is, that, when one comes
up, others do—and, as you yourself say, let's get together in Bostown.
It is a simple prop.: a man needs a lot o' woman, he needs, a lot of talk.
I can take a lot of, being alone, as I imagine you can. ((Slater was
wrong: us gregarious creatures (I don't know that Slater was, despite
all evidence, or Hart, for that matter)) Or at least, now, that things
have gone to worse, a man, to find out how much he is the only one,
needs such isolation as you practice. It is the same here, you will be
surprised to learn, or will you? I see no one, that is, in the city sense,
day on, out. And I like it—get work done. We have this small two
room jewel in brick, with garden, that, for four years now (we've been
here 7), I have been abt to lose monthly for non-payment of rent.
[*Added in margin:* 'Course, there the city is, outside the brick wall] I
leave the grass wild, and the gate is gone, and the bin has given way
from the rot. But the birds, bugs, cats, dogs like it—shit, screw, nest,
sing; and the Negroes, who used to drink muscatel down on the tracks
(B & O) a block away, now come in, that the gate's gone, and have
themselves a time, under the patched french windows 10 feet over their
head, where we sleep.

(The big struggle, after the decision to leave politics (THE K),[124] was to
leave Ez. I hunch that, more than that I am a hybrid, like WCW, or
that I purposely let him and madame think I was of fellows-jew, my
separating myself from him—and only two miles over the river—is the
pique. Plus the fact that certain workers (composer [Frank] Moore,
translator [Rudd] Fleming, young man [Eustace] Mullins) all, when
they have been in attendance on him, give him the sense of my pull as
well. That wld be fine, if he also saw me. But since that day I wrote
G[randPa] G[oodBye] (wot you and Leeds have, on him: date,
February, 1948) I have stayed away. And for the simplest reason: that

he was intervening between me and his work. And (as again, you) it's the work, only the work, that I, I who am alone alive, wanted.

Now, maybe, in a short while, I won't want it—in such an insistent sense.)

I was thinking of him, just now, with coffee, thinking abt the question you raise, where one works well, South or North, out of America or in (going on), how, in proof of what you say, how little any one else, past or present, effects the sense, "I, only," how it is only so now and then, that one even thinks, "here, in this same mud-flat, 3 of the only 4 fellow cits. I ever really took up from, have been: only Melville not, but Lincoln, Whitman, Pound. . ." And I jumped (by way of you, on Cino poems, London, 1910)[125] to Ez ("Shakespeare, fucked here? aw, piss"), to, in what force, is there any other men, EVEN THOSE WE LOVE.

I think, for ex., that I should not have liked, the skin of, Melville, Lawrence. (I do, the Old Man's!). I imagine I shld have liked S's. I did this, to explain it:

SO GENTLE

So gentle, nobody seems to have paid him much mind,
as they did Ben

so gentle, when he slipped off to Stratford he left no ripple
                                                            behind,
the Swan

Or Homer, who, after S, has had the largest influence on me (it sounds silly to say).

One plays this way, to invoke, a company.

To come back. What I wrote you yesterday on LINE, got neater, later. Maybe too neat. But here it is, just for the go of it, and because I think we do have to correct Remy de G and Ez, on this biz of, expression versus illumination. All the way thru I find em (including Ez's absolute

ARS POETICA) half right. (They leave out one side of the
thoroughfare, much-travelled side.)

At the moment—and maybe I'll go on, from PROVERSE, and do,
what I threatened myself, OPEN FIELD COMP.—it comes out like
this:

    the two halfs are,

        the HEAD, by way of the EAR, to the SYLLABLE,

        the HEART, by way of the BREATH, to the LINE

    And the joker: that the 1st half is, the let-it-rip, in the act,
           howsomever one disciplines it othertimes

        and the 2nd, is, the rewrite, the control, in the
        making, the *work of the day*

Hello, Creeley: this
is to greet you and,
to thank you, up there,
wherever it is, and in what light
you read it

      amo

       o

[Washington, D.C.
22 June 1950]
thursday (later, after yr
two letters, one on ADAMO,
other on MOOD, & EP)

You echo me, my lad. I took a turn. Got sick of all this recent push, figured it was worn out, was, as you say (say!), this, telling everybody. Fuck it. But god damn. (Go by the nose? Clean it, citizen.) Shit.

       Been off, now, for days, looking around, for another heave, something, say (will you say) Byzantine, like, or (again), Iranian. Okay.

       OK—and you see, we agree, Day/

                    diminutive.

                        OKAY. You,
and   I,   get on. [*Added in ink:*] (Want to throw at you, SHE-BEAR.)

NOW, as to MOOD and/or EP m ud and/or EP ode/ a./o/ WHO?

I dread the idea, frank, his name. Funny thing: was debating, between letter #1 today, and receiving your 2, whether to go further with you abt EZ, HIS ARs POETICA (it can be pulled out, did it, for myself, three years back—and damn good learnin', 'tis)
[*Added:* wot is not now noticed /in such a condensing, a
                    bringing together of, is
                    busting the METHOD/
                        is ANTHEIL, TREATISE,
                        HARMONIA][126]

Look: what abt this proposition (i can do the same for you, sd he). You got my letters. I ain't. Also, I trust bro. CREEL, as do the Others.

Now: if the fundamentals, WAS it, in that letter (was that, the
METHODOLOGY?)
          and add, on him against others, abt, SYLLABLES?
          (I mean, he goeth
                NOT BY HIS PERSONETH
                he goeth by
                langwitch)

PLUS yesterday-today, on *our* difference (you-me, he OLD G,
                                    for generation)

PLUS THIS:
      he,
      the biggest heave (so far, that is, at least, as
                the "Common Speech," its
                USES—de vulgare eloquentia)[127]
      since, Chaucer?

Anyhow, the correction of, the declaration by

"we have now in stock one CROWBAR, used, but,
crowbars do not deteriorate; EP, his brand, on handle"

THE TROCHEE:
                with it, a new language, for USE, made
                USA
(Where'd he get it, the trochee? hunch: out of Miss Sappho by
                          Seafarer

(And where, the single intelligence, to put his hand to it?

            hunch again (beside, of course, his
            native energy,
            WHITMAN, WHITMAN, WHITMAN, date,
            between, directly between, "Ripostes"
            and "Lustra," what 1912-13?
                        [Added in margin:

                                    Ezra/
                                    out of Whitman by/
                                    Homeros/]

          clue clue clue

[*Added:* ALSO, PLUS, PLUS, to limit same: he stays (standeth in the
     mind)
                    'CENTO MAN,
                              the same
                              NO LONGER GOOD ENUF]

Okay. The idea being,
as you on olson/ preface

                    as you on prose/ olson

                                        why not you on olson
                                        /on pound?

An idea. And not a duck, not ducking. Just this: that what's on
between us, is also a METHODOLOGY
                              (you pull out, i pull out)

     ((I like wot you say,
        &, specifically, hereon,
        "even a barer outline. . . the briefer, the better"

        —like you sd, for the MAG, you
          pull out Bud Berlin, fr. him, a letter))

This is a LIVE WAY.
                    Wot d'ya say?

In ency case, just
do whatever—and
it's okay with me. Only,
I shouldn't want, RIGHT NOW,
to step out of
the batter's box. I got my spikes in,
and it's here, the box, this
correspondence, you and me:
> what the fuck, MOOD? VARIEGATIONS (boy
> ain't that a pip?)? PNY (pnew)? or
> ferrini's drim, VOYAGER (ow)? Or
> GOOSEY GOOSE, for that matter?

for my dough, there'th
thee & me, and thee be. . .

ee be

o-el-es-o-en

p.s. 1:—by god, does the *Variegation* piece, mean no notice by R Cr
in MAG#1—did it, too, go out with (Leed's objection) all
"reviews"?

> by god, i regret that
> > it's the best g.d. notice this lad
> > hath had

PS 2: on NE:
> was, to have been there, this week,

BUT

(must write the Old Lady (Gloucester) right now, to
say, son not arriving YET)

Complicated reasons

Anyhow, usually jump, just because I'm a g.d. new englander, & think we're on this earth, not to enjoy ourselves.

Let me let you know, if / and when /
do jump. Certainly will be the coming
weeks—but, no better guess.

Two conditions of my nature which have permanently fucked me up:
I driving necessity to *act immediately* thereon, & whenever, wherever
    the notion comes (one's intimates, here, always, the problem)
II   *stasis*,   condition in which work gets done   (isolation, subtle
kinetic of flesh, so, *one* intimate)

PS 3: for the restatement of *yest. & today:*
               in poets,

                        the SYLLABLE the sign of
                          intelligence,
                        the LINE the sign of
                          heart

          &   poetics, forward, is
          a matter of, conspicuously,
          KINETICS, all over

[Washington, D.C.]
thurs. [22 June 1950]

look, r.c.:

this is developing under hand

I just opened this envelope. I had put in Gli Amanti, for the hell of it, again to give you something to think abt.

But now, I've opened it, in order to add DIRGE, & to ask your serious advice (if you don't mind:

tell you what it is— Emerson asked, as I think I told you, for *short* ones ("like those of y & x," he sd) for GG #1 (the anthology I shall push for, #2)

i'm castin' around, among the mss. It may be just today, BUT, would you say— & straight out, brother, yr my boy— WOT ABT these 2? Wld they do?

they ain't pot, but do they GOOF you?

Olson

p.s. be obliged, if, hot
    you'll give me yr word

[Washington, D.C.]
friday june 23 50

my dear c:

i never drew, on hart / don't know why / his life, yes, like him, special   it's of no importance, no measure whatsoever, but the verse, never did invoke me   tempted to think, simply because, feel so close to, the man   (queer, that way: never did, on HM, either, or lawrence, draw: just like 'em, like to think abt 'em, know: seems like, i go around collecting brothers, or whateverImakeem, in lieu of having same)   (anyhow, awful ignorant, abt other writers: somehow resist influence, except for those I mentioned to you yesterday) sure you're right on hart, for yrself (rather question, tho, relation hart-melville: if i had a demur on h c, i think it wld be, that, when he was, it was too late for him: already the body of this land was crocked   And her seas)

Did do, come to think of it, a verse on hart!   the 1st days i ever did same[128]   And it caused the most enigmatic business, between me and Marsden Hartley   I was heart-broken, for Hartley had found out my address on Christopher St (god, what a darling of a one-room house, with parquet-soapstoned floor, and me alone, for the 1st time in my life, trying to go to the mat with same) and, to my honor & surprise, come to see me in a new beautiful sea-green suit he'd bought, where I used to buy mine, my Harrises, at Macy's Made-To-Measure, 35 bucks! There he was, at my door! It was his peak, the 1st or 2nd Walker show, after his extraordinary 2nd birth (at 50, or so), the return to Maine.[129] And I was his. I was so nervous, I made tea, but it was only orange slices in hot water, I had forgotten to add the tea, and didn't know it, the cups were red Mexican clay, until he had gone. It went all right, until I pulled out, in my green enthusiasm, the Hart poem. He read it, slowly, sd no word, got up, took his hat, and walked out!

It has bothered me, since that day. Damned if I know, what went on. I still suffer over it.

Anyhow, what I wanted to say was, I called hart, new archeopteryx. And do have that feeling, that he was, somehow, some marvelous throw-back, a vestigia, forward, in that sense, surely. [*Added in ink:*] "To one of 'us' who does jump." Yes. I had it, this way: You who made a bridge / leaped

Agree, eloquent, as HM was, but think what you so accurately put, embarrassment, (& Bill also), (causeth), is actually that, what is the JOB, is to find a method (a logos, is it also to be called) OTHER THAN THE ELIZABETHAN, and what embarrasseth (Ezra, never) is the Elizabethan in

> melville, hart, & bill, sometimes, not very many times

(dry it out, boys, dry it out!)
((go to sea, citizens,

                    and find out))
(((Ahab was FULL STOP:[130] yr emperies, (how did you spill it?), are
   done for, end all thalassocracy: the ENERGY
   is elsewhere)))
                         and where it is,

                              is for us to find, for the likes of
you and me, ROBERT, grandson of, SEA-CAPTAINS!

            Signed   Olson, crew-member

[In ink, at top of page:]
p.s.   — wrote R. Emerson today, to say what about the olson
anthology for GG#2 (which would be 2-3-4 months *after* his next one,
early fall; & to thank him for welcoming me, via Creeley, Y&X, The
Kingfishers, & Cold Hell. Did not yet send smaller pieces he asks for, for
GG#1 (the fall one). [Troubled abt these shorter pieces.]

                                        [Washington, D.C.]
                                        friday [23 June 1950]

R Cr:

   I did forget to tell you, earlier today, the curious confirmation
   picked up last night, of my hunch of Ez vs O:

                                   we were out, one
   of those rare times, to spaghetti at Moore's, who sees the Kerekter
   once a week, the normal plan now that the K has settled down

around the waist and around the law

                                        Sez Moore, ''Yup, he
does, did take the Tale of Hines-Olson- Lybeck-Lubeck-
Hungarian-Gypsy-Jew, took it, hook, nose, line (bad) and sink
(who'z sunk)
                                BUT, sez Moore, wot Ez adds is,
this:
        ''Wot Olson don't know IZ,
        I hate Swedes as much as I do Jewz''

                                whoopz

                                        'allo, this is

                                O, a round
                                o, a very
                                earth, a very
                                (soil of) what
                                seed, & how many—aint
        it wonderful
                        to be multiple
                                to be
                                        just
                                        OLSON

[*Added in ink:*]
the which may well be again
another of those astounding
PERCEPTS of Ez, Kulch-wise:
for the truth is, as I begin
to find out (strzysgowski,[131] &
others), the ANTI-'CENTO (ANTI-MEDIT, ANTI-RENAISSANCE)
position does, amazingly, have
antecedents, stretching back thru Angle-England,
& Scandinavia, by way of Russia & Turkestan, to old Iran.

[*On back:*]
the *logos*   the word or form which expresses a thought,
                               also, the thought[132]

[Littleton, N.H.]
june 24, 50

Dear O/

Very goddam good of you, to take this trouble, and I got no kicks, none, nowhere. Everything fits, like you say. Well, to begin: let's take up the biz of the bit on prose. You are right/ abt the Freud. I was trying to get out, once in: and, how abt that: never thought of cutting the catch passage. Just that I was reading PG/ at the time/ and having been trapped, by myself, into the gig against Freud, wanted: OUT. So all that can go. As a matter of document: had got the ms/ out of the mailbox, to add the footnote, having been bedeviled by the lack of bearing, I had given it. So: you can take it/ it didn't sit well: at this end. Abt Payne (well, his taste really bugged me on the first issue—I mean, the southern biz: will that be constant?): no word from him yet, on it. Wd much rather the story go there/ than this: thinking yr idea about P/NY: a very good one. And wd like to see you hit this. You can. How are they for such things? To mean: I have had no truck with same, no stuff sent them, etc. And the biz: of 'authority' for such comment (as the bit on prose)—might bug them, by its lack. I have only my own opinion, i.e. Well, you say, & cd set abt retrieving same from Payne.

Now, the poems. Let's take the order they came in: all within this month. 1/ Poor Season: was the 'old' way—or simply, trying to find a method 'just' strong enough to hold the content, nothing more. I dont go with the sounds of it now/ much. The sense: oke, it's what I hang to. But wd/ make it more reach/ juxtaposition (image, etc.): if I cd get

back to it. Then: 2/ Littleton, N.H.—already, I'd cut (1) the
slogan—an irony that I am apt to get hung with, from embarrassment.
(2) Oddly, the temptation is to say the poem/ ends: with the first two
lines: but that is a irony: on: 'end.' I mean: we ride, to the end/ with
these things—what the push can sustain. In this one, I take the basicks
to be there. I am no surer than you are: that they are in their 'right'
order. That is the bug/ that the head is apt to go/ backwards: from the
'sign.' And to posit this in poetry: is to attempt a 'law' for reflection.
Well, subject to yr comment on the line-ing/ I wd let it stand for the
moment. Shifting, perhaps, the Kenneth part/ somehow: to its proper
locus. I do get yr point/ re the energy: lost by 'conserving' falsely, the
line. Better to shove & heave: where the logick IS rather than to let it
be a river: with strict banks. (Well, you are a good teacher—this is
clear.) Tho 'is the Fixer of Change . . . , ' for me, is not specific, is the
REAL drift. Is: 'change' (who can fix it, yet . . .) but that kind of
humor, is perhaps, too damn sly. I dont mean to be cute, in short.

3/ Slater poem. Many times, I orient myself, like they say: by my
beginnings/ and often: toss them out when I have done so. Many
stories: that way. You will note shiftings in any beginning of
anything: I send. I like all that you say abt this one. Real grip you have
on the headaches there. I had sent this to Emerson/ lacking else. He
has, too, the poor season/ but that is not it, the poetry. Littleton, I sent
to Imagi : who is a weak sort, or so I must think. Well, back to work on
that one/ tho you have done most of it. Abt the so-called 1st section: let
me go over it. Get back what was up, etc.

Now to other things: abt method/ the line. Well, to be straight with
you/ it's only my breathing, as I write. And the residue of the formal,
that hangs. I wd like someday, to write a line with this grip of stress:
Love god, we rather may, than either know him, or by speech utter
him.[133] You see? It is where the sound/sense: throws back forward: in
a 'real' logick. That is the kick. Well, it is the breath/ what you have
there. That makes the way. The head cannot shape a line more than the
ear can hear. Just, like they say, cant. Impossible. And the great
sounds concurrent with, say, the Eliz. lyricists, etc., was just that
method. I mean: say, with Shakespear: was ever a man going, more,
by his ear. Of course. The way. In the case of what's called 'strict

forms': simply the play within the external limit. Nothing different, in nature, etc., from the use in free verse et al.

Anyhow, I am at it. In these three months, or so: you've put down, by example, and straight speech: a whole logic for a line, attention to line. What others have said (the doc) but somehow haven't: quite made clear. The breathing. Well, some time will have for you: story: IN THE SUMMER—which is all that beat. I made it there: straight. Got the pitch. Well, so much for that.

Anyhow, again thanks & will be writing soon again. Have just seen 2 of bks put out by Emerson: real great press & printing job. You sd really get something from him on the collection.

Creeley

[*Added at top of letter:*]
when can i look for you/ word had it/ via vince/ you had already been???

They is singing: 'Pollyarchie . . .'

———

[Littleton, N.H.]
June 24 [1950]

O/

beat this out,[134] after whacking at the field with the neighbor's scythe. Am bushed. So, what do you think. Have sent it on to Payne. I know I dont get to much. (To speak true: I aint got the bk here, which is sortof/ a drag.) Had lent it to Leed & he hasnt got it back here yet. Well—it's an opening for the line biz. Was sorry to beat on the poor

chap I quote/ but dammit they ask for it: look what he lifts in 'O, etc.' :
and the line killing him. Sounds awful (& why did he bring it in on the
IN beat, phew) Well, so much for that. Hope Payne's agreeable to the
alias, & the piece. Sd be something sd. Eh,—sure.

yr lad/ C.

Wd you return this sometime/ only copy. Will be getting yr poems
back pronto. Ugh Ugh.

[Littleton, N.H.]
june 24 [1950]

O/

Perhaps a bastard to shove this on you.[135] My idea: you hold to
this copy, & if Payne dont want it, then wd you be good enough,
old sport, to send it to P/NY. I have a fear of them. Or with such
things, where I am trying to make sense, at least, for myself—I
hate to send it, anywhere. Odd, but so it is. You cd say to them:
no need to return ms/—just a card at their leisure, since it will be.
For document, if that's what pleases them: have the story coming
in KENYON this fall. (Not the greatest, but oke.) I have my
doubts on this ground: will P/NY, with their emphasis on poetry,
handle the prose biz—most obviously there is a relation, but will
they pick up on it? Well, what wd you think—I know nothing abt
them.   If you think best, tell Payne I sd to shoot back the
thing here/ and to consider, only, the story. Oke with me—as you
think it wd best go.

[*Added in pencil:*] All section headings *yr* words.

You will see the obvious changes, etc. Per yr suggestion, have put an addition (slight, or so: seeming) into the biz re: beginnings & ends. It's just that way I see it—that prose is: multiple presents. What hits back to: Dos/. What's happening: here. Say pp 4, 20, 150, 2000. What's in yr head/ at that mo: the logic. Prose's. Dont let noone tell yez different. The frame: is no less of a 'hanger' than the 'sonnet.' Well, that's the thought.

Abt my barbarity: it is. I know. But it is, also, : my joke, and for that yez will allow me to leave it. Obviously, sd yr lad, most slyly—the only way to get peoples heads to exacts—is to introduce barbarities, fer contrast, but

as time makes the logick/ it posits: its exacts,—& being the only logic fer prose/ gives the only exacts: time IS a progression ..... to stasis.

       But that's something else agin.

[Littleton, N.H.]
june 24 [1950]
aft

O/

       just a note while I got it/ i.e., yr letters (4) here this noon/ too much/ many thanks. You'll have my own gig on the line, etc., written just before this stuff slid in: how abt that. So: for the moment, the problem of the shorter poems. Well, looking thru these 2/ I take it: GLI AMANTI is a good bit beyond DIRGE. But I dont take it, either of them, got what MOVE OVER & LA CHUTE have got. But something like the GM/ slays me—but I got the benefit of yr letters, etc. What I'm going to do: sound out Leed on the biz of the two we have/ I mean: no use you shouldn't have them, failing other work. And we hung up/ at the mo/ as we are. The point/ should rather you let these go on to Emerson (MOVE OVER & LA CHUTE &, say, GLI AMANTI) and then keep with us in matters of head/ crit/ demonstration of direct objectives, to begin with the education biz. To mean: cd we, perhaps, look to you on something re that (educ/) for #2 (this fall)—and for things like/ reviews: brief, & general head work, that has to be done, to tie things in. I mean/ you know what I think of the 2 poems & knowing that, it dont matter AS much whether or not I print them, granted Emerson will. I think he will / not much doubt abt that. La Chute/ real crazy beats in that/ bongo. Too much: shows what yez can do with rhythms in an open form. I mean: a fine thing. MOVE OVER/ I put with yr best. So why sdn't Emerson pick up. Well, tell me what you think of that/ say: one bit on educa/ & 2 bottles beer for 2 poems & 3 goose eggs? Oke. I mean: tho I most certainly want to have the poetry (GOOD)—I can pick up bits here & there that go/ tho the makers of same, may be unable to push on the given head we pick. BUT to find someone like yrself, willing to go whole hog, and having the understanding & head—not everyday. So leave me to settle with Leed/ you send off those 3 to GG/ then think abt possible prose, to be tied-in to Education/ cd be coming for a fall issue. That seems the best thing all way round. You'll be making more of these good things & we'll be printing them. Just that you sd bear down on E/ while he's in the mood. Dont know what might happen, etc. Here, you do.

                                                            Sd note,
Master O/ yr use of 'description' in A Catharsis/ i.e., 'of the day & night, like a diner.'[136] U are right— it saps the energy. Heh heh.

Well, it is a nice thing, sure, but lacks the fullness of some like I've noted. & damned if I think it wd get it out of MY SYSTEM. heh heh. Do you know (sure) that fine poem by the doc, permeated with said heh heh heh?[137]

On reviews: per mag. Nothing tight there/ have yet to fight it out with L/ think he'll go with it. Want, certainly, a bit on yr little bk. My intention. Will do best/ granted HIS press & HIS money, etc. Oke?   Leed is cool/ dont worry.

Well, other things. Slater on the city: to be true—he had said, necessary that you get with those who are making things in yr own time, absolutely. He is right/ but it comes to: here we are doing it/ the distance be fucked, etc. Simply, that close to the city, in it, I went under: cd not hold myself/ or work. Just too damn much for me—i.e., THERE my own gregariousness had me right by the balls, like they say. I cd not LIVE with Ann, say, my wife. CD NOT. Just cdn't stay in the same room comfortably. Felt, always, that I was in some sense, being cheated. I.e., had drunk for a time prior to marriage, & then after. A rough biz. Not all the way gone, but shot: ¾ of any day. Not good. I.e., how can yez work under said conditions. You cant even think abt it/ all shades & movements: outside. Nothing in: but muck. So, we moved the works to the Cape. Worse. I mean: cd not sit still/ wanted to get back all the time. Wd be sitting down & then: just go. Back 2 or 3 days later/ CD NOT sit still. So, up here, & after working, getting the place somewhat back in shape/ being pinched for loot/ no money for likker, etc., : got cool again. I mean: cd work: & everything of use, thinking, or demonstration, begins there. This winter, because of the cold & money to heat the place, tho small, thought of moving to NY/ but stayed. Expect we'll be here for some time. TOO—it was that in the city, those I cd see: were useless/ dead. Pointless to talk to them, etc. NOT egoism/ simply cdn't see what they saw or they what I saw, etc. Well, so much for that.

I will try the bit on Ez' method, using yr notes. I had thought of that, but then: thought since you had written them, you cd do the job a hell of a lot better. But enough/ I expect, if I can just get the groundsense of that method: across, as you have documented it, etc. Will try & show you what comes of it. Cant yet get to it/ a couple of weeks, & can. They dont need it right away. Can make use of his notes/ re the economics: they want something on that head too. Will think it over: nothing so damned important at that. (But hope to god no one ever asks me to explain, or 'amplify'— the end.)

To be a shit/ like you had it there: two conditions of yr nature: …. go or stay: what else.

jump/ settle: same thing.

Will be looking for you, whenever you can make it. If you can, give me a couple of days notice. But when you can. Will get down. Just this biz with Leed has me/ straight out. Somewhat confused. It may be that he can handle it from his end/ with help there (friends or what). I hate to make that trip what with our finances, etc., being what they are. Boston/ yes. But the others are beyond my reach at the moment. Slater due here, he thinks, sometime in July/ but no definite word. I dont think he'd give a shit, if I slipped out for a day or two. So say when you know.

Do you know that the Harvard Bulletin is the favorite reading of over 12,000 paid subscribers?' Somewhat of a shock to think abt that. (I dont get it, myself.)

Variegation: preetttty hopeless. I had just sent that to them for my own kicks/ had another bit with Leed, as I had said. Say/ how wd Payne take to a review (longer) of yr little bk for his pages? (he cd sure USE it . . .) (I mean: cd snake in all this biz we've been talking abt . . . wd be cool).

> For now/ yr lad:
>
> > Creeley

[*Added at top of last page:*]
(wife snoozin on the sofa/ dog under the table: little boy upstairs—pretty cool, I'd say.)

Some nota/ ah.

I.e., some of these warm days, you sd be picking up on, say, they sd: New Sounds—I mean, say, as of this mo/ am sitting here listening to some (real) nice things. Well, it is the matters of time (1) and variation (2): that cd interest you. It is not to suggest that a logos (this) can be jumped to a logos (that)—but there are parallels. Many times have thought (tho not without blindness) if, say, if: I cd put down a series of lines, that wd string themselves, like the lines/line: in Bach (back/ & back): well/ wd be one sweet biz. Now with the matter at hand—here is the gig. The Bird (also Chas) has strung his way thru abt (now) 30

variations (on wax) of the one I GOT RHYTHM (agreed)—where we
have, as you will know, a series of (basick) chords which can be
extended in a strict (gripped) manner, inverted, wound, pitched, &
heaved, or let's just—go. so we go, like: la   do   de   da : becomes
oo   oo   de   la   oo/ (oo) da ee oo/ (different but the same: like
Coleridge, yet). Well, it is something to hear, old sport, if against yr
ear you is placing, are, the basic sounds/ then these: well, back in
Burma, sipping my—tea. But timing: there we can learn, right from
the pattern, without more (ado). There is nothing being put down that
can match/ that timing: Bird's. It is: flight/ on sound & sense. Good
stuff. Well, cant say more, except that you wd do well/ to stay clear of :
bop/ usual shit. It aint the thing (the same thing)—but like the biz of
the (   ) it was bird taught me. And, to be true, the phrase like here, it
is, is no different : from there/ the same, a, a: push & sense, of: limit.

Well, to orient yrself: wd suggest you listen to any of the following.

Miles Davis: Boplicity & reverse side.
  "   " :   Move.
The Bird   :   Chasing the Bird   i got
           :   Cheryl   ryhtmethe, . . .
           :   Dont Blame Me
           :   Donna Lee   I got R/
           :   Billy's Bounce   & so on? yes. There are a
                              great many/ but each of the
                              above: sd do it.

The names to look for/ whenever getting this type:
                         musick/

Miles Davis, Chas Parker, Bud Powell, Max Roach, Milt Jackson, Al
Haig, &c.
                 But the above/ all yez know: on earth
                 & all yez need: to know: to leave it.

me, i got eyes for asia.
(how you come on)

[*Added at top of page:*]
(later: perhaps not it/ but: for document and //: you will know/ that
what makes the LINE in any of this, IS, most obviously, the breath—it
is a profitable analogy, for the problems of poesy, or—just so/ the bird/
within the limit of his sounds/ breath/ is attempting to reach to: form/
from content: just so/ you/I: with our sound/ sense: and TIME. It is
interesting, as document, to cite his KNOWING of the problem. Tho it
is assumed that all jazz (uh huh) has a (uh huh) beat.. (uh huh).
Hmmm. . . . Well, so has mary had er has: a little lamb: I look to
EXTENSIONS.)

Notes

1 William Carlos Williams wrote Olson on 20 April 1950: "Drop a note to Robert Creely [*sic*], Littleton, N.H.—he's got some ideas and wants to USE them. Maybe you've already heard of him. Write. Send him anything you think is worth perpetuating." The *"PROjective Verse vs. the NONprojective"* is an early version of the famous "Projective Verse" essay, which would appear—with revisions resulting from the coming exchange with Creeley—in the magazine *Poetry New York* in October 1950.

As part of the background to this correspondence, the reader may also wish to see Creeley's letters to Vincent Ferrini, in George F. Butterick, "Creeley and Olson: The Beginning," *Boundary* 2, 6/7 (Spring-Fall 1978), 129-34. Also, Jacob Leed, "Robert Creeley and *The Lititz Review:* A Recollection with Letters," *Journal of Modern Literature,* 5 (April 1976), 243-59.

2 William Carlos Williams, "With Forced Fingers Rude," *Four Pages,* no. 2 (Feb. 1948), 1-4—an attack on Eliot for embracing Milton.

3 T. David Horton, frequent visitor to Ezra Pound at St. Elizabeths Hospital and, later, co-publisher with John Kasper of the Square Dollar series of Poundian texts. Donald J. Paquette was a poet recommended to Creeley along with Horton by Pound (see the excerpt from Pound's letter, *Agenda,* 4, no. 2 [Oct.-Nov. 1965], 16).

4 Judson Crews (b. 1917), poet living in Taos, N.M.; also writing under the pseudonym Mason Jordan Mason.

5 Wallace Stevens in a symposium on "The State of American Writing, 1948," *Partisan Review,* 15 (Aug. 1948), 885.

6 Confucius' *Unwobbling Pivot & The Great Digest,* translated by Ezra Pound and issued as *Pharos* (Norfolk, Conn.), no. 4 (Winter 1947).

7 From "A Ballad upon a Wedding" by John Suckling.

8 From Olson's "La Préface" in *Y & X* (*Archaeologist of Morning,* New York, 1973, p. [43]).

9 Immanuel Velikovsky (1895-1979), whose *Worlds in Collision* was

159

published in April of that year. Excerpts appearing in *Collier's* magazine—"The Heavens Burst," 25 Feb. 1950, pp. 24ff., and "World on Fire," 25 March 1950, pp. 24ff.—had been read by Olson and are preserved among his papers.

[10] Ruth Benedict, "Psychological Types in the Cultures of the Southwest," in *Proceedings of the Twenty-Third International Congress of Americanists* (New York, 1930), p. 577. The passage is marked in Olson's copy.

[11] See Ezra Pound, Cantos 74 and 80 of *The Pisan Cantos* (New York, 1948), and note to Olson's June 9th letter below. The "mister simpson" is Dallam Simpson of Galveston, Texas, editor of the Pound-inspired *Four Pages* and an author of the "Cleaners' Manifesto" referred to in the letters to come.

[12] Josef Albers (1888-1976), the painter and rector of Black Mountain College from 1939 to 1949. He had hired Olson in 1948 to take Edward Dahlberg's place as a teacher of writing at the college (see, e.g., Martin Duberman, *Black Mountain*, New York, 1972, pp. 307-08).

[13] Author and friend of Olson (his *Zero, the Story of Terrorism*, published that year, was dedicated to Olson and his wife Constance); then teaching at Alabama College in Montevallo, Alabama, and editing the *Montevallo Review*, where Olson would first publish "The Kingfishers" and other work.

[14] In Eliot's poem "The Dry Salvages." "Omeliot" probably as in "O. M. Eliot," how Olson has it in "Projective Verse" (Eliot was awarded England's Order of Merit in 1948). Our Lady of Good Voyage, whose statue overlooks Gloucester Harbor, is the muse of *The Maximus Poems*.

[15] Unpublished, it is titled "The Mystery of What Happens When It Happens" and is a longer version—written in January 1950—of a lecture with the same title given at Black Mountain during Olson's first appearances there in the fall of 1948. See also his June 24 letter, where the piece is described as "center to a job on H[erman] M[elville], and the King James Version."

16 Periodical devoted to art and literature, edited in New York by Ruth and John Stephan from 1947 to 1949.

17 Rimbaud writes in a letter to Georges Izambard, [13] May 1871, that the poet arrives at the unknown by "le dérèglement de *tous les sens*," and again to Paul Demeny, 15 May 1871, "Le Poète se fait *voyant* par un long, immense et raisonné *dérèglement* de *tous les sens*."

18 In his "Letter to an Australian Editor," *Briarcliff Quarterly*, 3, no. 11 (Oct. 1946), p. 207, Williams writes: "Destruction, according to the Babylonia order of creation, comes before creation. Look it up. The same today. We must be destructive first to free ourselves from forms accreting to themselves tyrannies we despise."

19 From Stendhal's *Life of Henri Brulard*, trans. Catherine Alison Phillips (New York, 1925), p. 360, which Creeley had read that February (letter to Jacob R. Leed, 9 Feb. 1950). Also quoted in "Notes for a New Prose" (written ca. June 1950), in *A Quick Graph*, ed. Donald Allen (San Francisco, 1970), p. 17.

20 Actually the opening of William Carlos Williams' poem "Apology," in his *Complete Collected Poems* (New York, 1938), p. 35 (see Creeley's letter of ca. May 28 below).

21 Presumably among the selections from Pound's letters to Creeley published in *Agenda*, 4 (1965), 14-21. Those letters also present the "program" to which Creeley responds in the excerpt from his letter to Pound following.

22 Gordon Ringer, a California lawyer; another of Pound's recommendations, along with Horton and Paquette.

23 Manifesto by a group identifying itself as "the Cleaners" and signed D[allam] Simpson, L. C. Flynn, and Igon Tan, in *Four Pages*, no. 3 (March 1948), 3. It consists of the following points: "1. We must understand what is really happening. 2. If the verse-makers of our time, are to improve on their immediate precursors, we must be vitally aware of the duration of syllables, of melodic coherence, and of the tone leading of vowels. 3. The function of poetry is to debunk by lucidity."

24 From Williams' "Letter to an Australian Editor," p. 208.

²⁵ From Remy de Gourmont's letter to Ezra Pound, 13 June 1915, in response to Pound's "first plans for establishing some kind of periodical to maintain communications between New York, London and Paris" (quoted in Pound's *Make It New*, New Haven, 1935, pp. 330-31).

²⁶ "In Cold Hell, In Thicket," described in Olson's postcard later that day as an "antey-dantey," i.e. anti-Dante.

²⁷ Gene Magner, editor of the magazine *Glass Hill* in Buffalo from 1949 to 1950. Vincent Ferrini had sent him a prose piece by Olson (possibly "The Resistance"), which he rejected, and Olson himself sent "The Morning News," which Magner returned that April saying he had too much material accepted for the magazine, although inviting Olson to try again in a few months.

²⁸ Kitasono Katue (b. 1902), Japanese poet and editor of the magazine *Vou* from Tokyo, whose poem "A Shadow" appeared in *Four Pages*, no. 6 (June 1948). See Olson's brief note on him in *Right Angle* for May 1949.

²⁹ Constantine Poulos, who had been Olson's director at the OWI during the war until 1944, when both he and Olson resigned (see "Two OWI Aides Resign: Poulos and Olson charge interference, but director denies it," *New York Times*, 19 May 1944, p. 14). Subsequently, as Balkan correspondent for the Overseas News Agency, he reported regularly on developments in Greece for the *Nation* and *New Republic* from 1947 to 1951.

³⁰ The spring 1950 issue of the *Hudson Review* was devoted in part to Ezra Pound and included his translation of *The Analects* of Confucius, selections from his letters to Eliot on *The Wasteland* and to W. H. D. Rouse on translating Homer, and an article by Hugh Kenner on *The Cantos*.

³¹ "Letter to an Australian Editor," in a special Williams issue of the *Briarcliff Quarterly* (see note 18 above).

³² See "Henry James and Remy de Gourmont," in Pound, *Make It New*, pp. 251-333. De Gourmont (1858-1915), French literary critic and novelist, was one of the founders of the *Mercure de France* and a spokesman for the symbolist movement.

[33] See Walter Pater, *The Renaissance: Studies in Art and Poetry* (London, 1935), pp. 40 and 43-44.

[34] E. E. Cummings' novel of imprisonment in France during World War I, published in 1922.

[35] From Hart Crane, "The Hurricane," in *Collected Poems* (New York, 1933), p. 124.

[36] An essay by Paul Goodman, in *Kenyon Review*, 7 (Autumn 1945), 628-44.

[37] From Chaucer's "Nun's Priest's Tale" (l. 3166), used by Olson in "GrandPa, GoodBye," in *Charles Olson & Ezra Pound*, ed. Catherine Seelye (New York, 1975), p. 101.

[38] Cf. Pound's definition of *logopoeia*—one of the "three 'kinds of poetry'"—as "the dance of the intellect among words," in "How to Read," *Polite Essays* (Norfolk, Conn., [1940]), p. 170. In writing "hard as a youth" six lines below, Olson alludes to Canto 80, where Pound writes, "I have been hard as youth sixty years" (*Pisan Cantos*, p. 91).

[39] "Mrs Metcalf told me she saw the truism pasted under the cover of his black desk: Keep true to, the dreams of, your youth"—Olson in notes toward the essay "Equal, That Is, to the Real Itself," 1958, among his papers.

[40] Pound to Eliot, an anecdote recorded earlier by Olson in "David Young, David Old," written late 1948 or early 1949 (in *Human Universe and Other Essays*, ed. Donald Allen, New York, 1967, p. 107).

[41] Probably "For Sappho, Back," an early version of which is dated 25 May 1950, or the unfinished "Help Me, Venus, For You Have Led Me On," from this same period.

[42] Latin *potentia*, "power."

[43] Creeley's story "The Unsuccessful Husband," eventually published in *Kenyon Review*, 13 (Winter 1951), 64-71, but see Creeley's 20 Sept. 1950 letter and note.

[44] See "Twelve Japanese Poets" in *Quarterly Review of Literature*—edited by Theodore Weiss (Creeley puns on the German "know-

nothing")—4 (1948), 343-45 and contributor's note on p. 400.

45 Echoes Whistler to Wilde: "I wish I had said that." "You will, Oscar, you will." (Attributed by *Oxford Dictionary of Quotations* to L. C. Ingleby, *Oscar Wilde*, p. 67.)

46 H. S. M. Coxeter, *Non-Euclidean Geometry* (Toronto, 1942), p. 10, quotes the Hungarian mathematician Bolyai Farkas (1775-1856) concerning discoveries of his son Janos that he intended to include as an appendix to his own book: "many things have an epoch, in which they are found at the same time in several places, just as the violets appear on every side in spring." Referred to by Olson on a number of other occasions, e.g. "The Story of an Olson" and "Apollonius of Tyana."

47 Originally reported by Max Eastman in his *Literary Mind: Its Place in an Age of Science* (New York and London, 1935), p. 100: "to something that I said Joyce answered in exactly these words: 'The demand that I make of my reader is that he should devote his whole life to reading my works.' He smiled as he said that—smiled, and then repeated it."

48 German *also*, "thus; therefore," and *wieder*, "again, once more." I.e., *und so weiter*, "and so forth."

49 See also "Reading at Berkeley," *Muthologos*, ed. George F. Butterick (Bolinas, Calif., 1978), I, 131: "I got myself called a Semite by telling Ezra Pound that my grandmother's name was Lybeck, which is obviously Lubeck . . ." Michael Lekakis, who reported Pound's remarks, was a sculptor living in New York. The last phrase is from Shakespeare's sonnet 129: "bait / On purpose laid to make the taker mad."

50 I.e., at Saint Elizabeths Hospital across the Anacostia, where Pound was interned. In a letter to Olson, 18 February 1950, Williams had referred to Pound as "the old gopher or wombat or wolverine (part skunk)."

51 Olson writes in "GrandPa GoodBye," *Charles Olson & Ezra Pound*, p. 97: "'30 yrs, 30 yrs behind the time'—you hear it from him, over and over. It is his measure (and his rod) for all work, and men. His mind bursts from the lags he sees around him." To the younger Pound,

writing in "The Teacher's Mission," *Polite Essays*, p. 120, the delay was not quite so long: ". . . the 15 to 20 years' delay with which all and every idea, and every new kind of literature, reaches the 'American reader' or 'teacher.'" See also Creeley's May 22 letter, and Olson's of May 25.

52 Eleanor Baron, a friend of Creeley's from Cambridge, Mass.

53 Pound writes of "Criticism by exercise in the style of a given period" in "Date Line," *Make It New*, p. 3, and discusses problems of translation in the essays, "Translations of Greek" and "Cavalcanti," in that volume, pp. 125-56 and esp. 398-407.

54 From "The Everlasting Gospel," in *Poetry and Prose of William Blake*, ed. Geoffrey Keynes, 4th ed. (London, 1948), p. 136. The quotation following is from Blake's *Descriptive Catalogue*, written for his drawing of "The Penance of Jane Shore" (*Poetry and Prose*, p. 618).

55 From Wallace Stevens' "Connoisseur of Chaos," in his *Parts of a World* (New York, 1942), p. 49.

56 The phrase is Pound's, most immediately for Creeley in a letter from him (see *Agenda*, 4, 1965, p. 19). See also Creeley's 1 June 1950 letter to Olson.

57 Henri Alain-Fournier's novel, first published in 1913 and available in Françoise Delisle's translation.

58 John Berryman's poems "The Long Home" and "Narcissus Moving," in *The Dispossessed* (New York, 1948), pp. 92-94 and 100-01. The lines quoted below are from his poem concerning Pound entitled "The Cage," appearing in *Poetry*, 75 (Jan. 1950), 187-88.

59 From Wallace Stevens' "So-and-So Reclining on her Couch," in *Transport to Summer* (New York, 1947), p. 15.

60 See Pound's footnote in his essay on Henry James in *Make It New*, pp. 288-89.

61 Pound, in "Hugh Selwyn Mauberley," *Personae* (New York, [1949]), p. 187.

62 In his *Journals*, trans. Justin O'Brien (New York, 1948), II, 276,

André Gide writes: "I think that *The Idiot* is particularly likely to please the young, and of all Dostoyevsky's novels it is the one I should advise them to read first."

[63] From Pound's "Mauberley" (*Personae*, p. 188).

[64] David Rousset's *L'Univers Concentrationaire* (Paris, 1946), an account of his experiences in the Buchenwald concentration camp, had been issued as *The Other Kingdom* in the United States by Olson's publisher, Reynal & Hitchcock, the same year as *Call Me Ishmael*. Rousset's *Les Jours de Notre Mort* (Paris, 1947) was a fictionalized version of the same experiences. Louis Martin-Chauffier, too, wrote of his sufferings in the horror camps in *L'Homme et La Bête* (Paris, 1947), a copy of which was in Olson's library. The works may have been known to Olson through his friend Jean Riboud, himself a survivor of Buchenwald and for whom Olson wrote "The Resistance." Joe Gould (1889?-1957) was a Greenwich Village literary figure, author of the legendary but lost *Oral History of Our Time*.

[65] Xenophon, whose *Memorabilia* or "Recollections of Socrates," like the *Dialogues of* Plato, presents a record of Socrates' conversations.

[66] Clarence H. Graham (1906-1971), a specialist in visual perception, whom Olson knew when both taught at Clark University in 1934-36. See also *Letters for Origin*, ed. Albert Glover (New York, 1970), p. 7.

[67] Anthropologist Ruth Benedict (1887-1948), whose acquaintance Olson had briefly made in Washington when both worked for the OWI. See her *Tales of the Cochiti Indians* (Washington, 1931).

[68] A short story by Rexford Stead, whom Olson had met through Robert Payne, in the *Montevallo Review*, no. [1] (Summer 1950), 33-40.

[69] Possibly *viva voce*, during one of Olson's visits to Ford Madox Ford in New York (arranged through Edward Dahlberg) or at a gathering of The Society of Friends of William Carlos Williams in 1939, which Ford founded (see Williams' *Autobiography*, New York, 1951, p. 301) and of which Olson was a charter member.

[70] From *The Ghost of Abel* (*Poetry and Prose*, p. 584).

[71] See William Carlos Williams' introduction to *The Wedge* (1944) in *Collected Later Poems* (Norfolk, Conn., 1950), p. 5: "It isn't what he says that counts as a work of art, it's what he makes, with such intensity of perception that it lives with an intrinsic movement of its own to verify its authenticity. Your attention is called now and then to some beautiful line or sonnet-sequence because of what is said there. So be it. To me all sonnets say the same thing of no importance." Creeley writes in "A Note on Poetry," *A Quick Graph*, p. 26: "When Williams beats on the sonnet, and he has done it I think brilliantly—he is hitting at a usage which denies form *now*. In short—that implies we ourselves are incapable—as our predecessors were of course *not*—of invention, of finding in the direct context of what we know, where we are, an exact means to form—which will be the direct issue of such contact. The sonnet says, in short, we must talk, if you want, with another man's mouth, in the peculiar demands of that 'mouth,' and can't have our own."

[72] André Gide, midway through *The Counterfeiters*, trans. Dorothy Bussy (New York, 1927), pp. 204-05. Quoted by Creeley also in a letter to Jacob Leed, ca. 17 January 1949.

[73] *The Paintings of D. H. Lawrence* (London, 1929). Olson had apparently written, in a letter now lost, of his acquisition of a collection of Lawrence first editions from a Washington bookseller that spring. Included was an original watercolor by Lawrence of a man urinating on daffodils.

[74] Both passages are from Lawrence's letter of 12 February 1915 to Russell, in *D. H. Lawrence's Letters to Bertrand Russell*, ed. Harry T. Moore (New York, 1948), pp. 31 and 33; also in *Atlantic*, 182 (Dec. 1948), p. 94.

[75] Francis J. Thompson, author of "Courageous, Not Outrageous" in *Hopkins Review*, 3 (Summer 1950), 42-44, a review of *New Directions* 11.

[76] From a conversation between Midwestern racketeers in James M. Cain's *Love's Lovely Counterfeit* (New York, 1942). The quotation is actually: "Wise money has generally got Illinois plates" ("wise money" in the sense of belonging to those "in the know").

[77] From the fifteenth-century "Lament for the Makers," by Scottish poet William Dunbar.

[78] Probably from Creeley's unpublished story "Leonardo's Nephew," written in the summer of 1948 (see his June 13 letter).

[79] Sent Jacob Leed ca. 10 August 1949 with the comment: "enclosed please find poem and will say this much, between you and me, there is no such photograph or there may be but I have not seen it but still it will be fun to see in the years to come all of the fans going out of their minds in vain endeavor to locate same and I am not the one to banish joy."

[80] Sent Jacob Leed ca. 5 November 1949 with a letter in which Creeley says: "For Looie, that is Simpson, have written the SONGE," quoting "roughe windes doe shakee theee the darlinge ofe mee hearte . . . ," an echo of Shakespeare's sonnet 18.

[81] From an earlier letter of Olson's, now lost; used along with other quotations from the same letter to introduce sections of Creeley's "Notes for a New Prose" (*A Quick Graph*, p. 12).

[82] See Creeley's April 28 letter and note 5 above.

[83] This is the first appearance of this famous formula, incorporated by Olson in "Projective Verse" (*Human Universe*, p. 52).

[84] Paul Goodman, *The Dead of Spring* (Glen Gardner, N.J., 1950), p. 11.

[85] A reprint of Alexander Del Mar's *History of Monetary Crimes*, published by the Cleaners' Press (Washington, D.C., 1950) as part of their Square $ series.

[86] Jakob Wasserman (1873-1934), Austrian novelist. His novel *The World's Illusion* (1920), especially, has suggested comparisons to Dostoyevsky.

[87] Williams writes in *Paterson* (New York, 1948), p. 46: "Who restricts knowledge? . . . And if it is not / the knowledgeable idiots, the university, / they at least are the non-purveyors / should be devising means / to leap the gap."

[88] Fabrizio del Dongo, principal character of Stendhal's *Charterhouse of Parma*.

89 From Miller's "Mademoiselle Claude," *The Wisdom of the Heart* (Norfolk, Conn., 1941), p. 140. Other references are to his "Reunion in Brooklyn," in *Sunday After the War* (Norfolk, Conn., 1944), pp. 63-106; "Via Dieppe-Newhaven," in *The Cosmological Eye* (Norfolk, Conn., 1939), pp. 197-228; and his correspondence with Michael Fraenkel, *Hamlet*, 2 vols. ([New York], 1939-41). Fraenkel (1896-1957), a friend of Miller's, was the author of *Death Is Not Enough* (London, 1939), as well as *Death in a Room* (New York, 1936) and *Bastard Death* (Paris and New York, 1946).

90 Pound's three-line poem "Papyrus" (*Personae*, p. 112), which concludes "Gongala . . . . . . ," an allusion to one of Sappho's disciples as found in Suidas. Glenn Hughes, *Imagism and the Imagists* (Stanford, 1931), p. 123, suggests the poem is "a satire on H. D. and her Sapphics."

91 "La Préface," reprinted in *Vou* (Tokyo), no. 33 (1949), 35.

92 *Imagi*, no. 13 (1950), edited by Thomas Cole in Allentown, Pa., an issue entitled "Mid-Century American Poetry (A Celebration)." Included was "These Days" by Olson, two poems by Judson Crews, and work by Cummings, Pound, Marianne Moore, Stevens, and Williams.

93 Olson's adaptation of "Lament for the Makers" reached only nine stanzas. In it, he translates the refrain "Timor mortis conturbat me"—from the Office of the Dead—as both "The fear of death deranges me" and, as further along in this letter, "The fear of death confoundeth me."

94 The ant and centaur occur together in Pound's famous image in Canto 81, in *Pisan Cantos*, p. 99.

95 From Olson's poem "Move Over" (see Creeley's May 26 letter).

96 Freud's *Moses and Monotheism*, trans. Katherine Jones (New York, 1939), which Olson had found useful for *Call Me Ishmael*.

97 Jean Riboud.

98 Actually reflects a dispute in Washington at the time over forced radio listening on public buses and streetcars. The *New York Times*, 14 April 1950, p. 25, reports: "Two bus users who do not like music while they ride filed suit today in an effort to shut off the mobile radio broadcasts on the Capital Transit Company's vehicles. They asked the United States

District Court to reverse to [*sic*] decision of the Public Utilities Commission that it was all right for the transit company to furnish its passengers with the musical fare plus news and advertising. The appeal was made by Franklin L. Pollak and Guy Martin [on behalf of a 500-member organization called the Transit Riders Association], who said the broadcasts made it difficult for them 'to read and converse and deprived them of their privacy.'" The suit was dismissed, however, by the Federal court (see *New York Times*, 2 June 1950, p. 46). See also *Maximus* I, 3 and 13.

This letter serves as the basis for Olson's poem "ABCs (3—for Rimbaud)," which had been sent, as "For Arthur Rimbaud," to Frances Boldereff the same day, although dated (perhaps erroneously?) June 8.

99 All elements to be found in Pound's *Pisan Cantos*, as are Dioces (first king of the ancient Medes), the goddess Artemis, and others mentioned below.

100 Pound, Canto 80 (*Pisan Cantos*, p. 89): "La beauté, 'Beauty is difficult, Yeats' said Aubrey Beardsley / when Yeats asked why he drew horrors . . .''

101 From Canto 83 (*Pisan Cantos*, p. 107).

102 From Chaucer's "Nun's Priest's Tale" (l. 3164), used in "GrandPa GoodBye," *Olson & Pound*, p. 101.

103 William Carlos Williams, *In the American Grain* (Norfolk, Conn., [1948]), pp. 105ff., concerning the circle of writers and artists in the Paris of the Twenties.

104 See also *Contexts of Poetry: Interviews 1961-1971*, ed. Donald Allen (Bolinas, Calif., 1973), p. 157. Phillips (1811-1884) was an American social reformer.

105 "The Kingfishers," published in the Summer 1950 issue of the *Montevallo Review*, edited by Robert Payne.

106 Richard Wirtz Emerson (b. 1924), editor of Golden Goose Press. See Creeley's May 26 letter.

107 Robert Payne, "A Note on Two Poems by Mao-Tse-Tung," *Nine*, 1 (Autumn 1949), 18-20.

108 Creeley's poem "Hart Crane," dedicated to Slater Brown (in *For*

Love: Poems 1950-1960, New York, 1962, pp. 15-16). "Littleton, N.H." is collected in *The Charm: Early and Uncollected Poems* (San Francisco, 1969), pp. 24-25.

[109] Poem by Karl Shapiro, collected in his *V-Letter and Other Poems* (New York, 1944), pp. 42-46.

[110] From "La Préface" (*Archaeologist of Morning,* p. [43]). "The Burning Babe" is probably "The Babe / the Howling Babe," also in that poem, rather than Robert Southwell's sixteenth-century poem.

[111] Poem by Hart Crane, in his *Collected Poems,* p. 126.

[112] An early version of the poem "Adamo Me" (*Archaeologist of Morning,* pp. [21]-[26]). On the manuscript, which Creeley returned, he comments (opposite section beginning "both beauty AND / eternity"): "this seems to me NO LESS 'description' or loss of energy—Should be BIG—SINGLE—than like, mighty like—a rose." Again, in section towards the end beginning "(as they lay, in that roaring . . . ," he writes: "this is SOUND you lack earlier."

[113] A quarterly edited in St. Louis by G. Wendleton and T. Trova. Issue no. 23 (May 1950) featured work by and about Pound.

[114] Theodore Spencer (1902-1949), professor at Harvard and poet, visitor to Pound (see *Olson & Pound,* pp. 87-89). Pound had said the same thing in a letter to his lawyer, Julien Cornell, quoted in *The Trial of Ezra Pound* (New York, 1966), p. 71: "Olson saved my life. Young doctors absolutely useless—must have 15 minutes sane conversation daily."

[115] In Crane's *Collected Poems,* pp. 93-99.

[116] *Isabelle,* a *"récit"* by Gide, in his *Two Symphonies,* trans. Dorothy Bussy (New York, 1931).

[117] "I was so caught up/ in the afflatus of that season"—"The Morning News," *Archaeologist of Morning,* p. [110].

[118] I.e., Creeley's "Littleton, N.H."—although as rewriting by Olson of that poem under the title "Creeley, N.H." survives among his papers.

[119] Unpublished poems. "Iranian" in the sense of Indo-European or "ANTI-MEDIT[ERRANEAN], ANTI-RENAISSANCE" (see Olson's

second June 23 letter, p.147). Creeley's "The Poor Season," mentioned on p. 124, likewise has never been published.

120 Pound's definition of *logopoeia*. See Olson's May 25 letter and note 38 above.

121 Golden Goose Chap Book no. 9 (Columbus, O., 1950), with a lead article on the state of American poetry by Richard Wirtz Emerson and Frederick Eckman entitled "The Crisis." Emerson's *Five Poets* mentioned shortly below is Golden Goose Chap Book no. 5, *Five Poets: Robert L. Beum, Leslie W. Hedley, Harold G. Miller, Scott Greer, Nathan R. Teitel* (Columbus, O., 1949).

122 Another copy sent Jacob Leed and signed, in jest, "Karl Shapiro." The "Louis" in lines 60 and 63 is undoubtedly Louis Simpson, whom Creeley mocks in letters to Leed from 1949 and 1950.

123 From Blake's "When Klopstock England defied . . . ," *Poetry and Prose*, p. 104.

124 The poem from *Y & X* (*Archaeologist of Morning*, p. [9]) that contains Olson's "answer"—his decision to renounce politics as a career.

125 Pound's "Cino," after the Italian poet Cino da Pistoia, first published in *A Lume Spento* (Venice, 1908) and again in *Personae* (pp. 6-7). Olson refers to it in "GrandPa GoodBye" as a beautiful poem of love (*Olson & Pound*, p. 100), and himself wrote a poem entitled "Cinos," dated 18-19 April 1950 but unpublished.

126 Pound's *Antheil and the Treatise on Harmony* (Paris, 1924).

127 Dante's treatise on the vernacular tongue, *De vulgari eloquentia*, which sought to establish Italian as a literary language equal to Latin.

128 A poem entitled "Space" from ca. 1946, which begins:
> Space was your shroud and swaddle,
> transcontinental blood of Indian girl
> beat of your dream. Fledged by the modern
> new Archeopteryx, you Hart Crane
> drank the poison as Crockett the cloud . . .

In another poem, likewise unpublished, the lines appear as: "New

Archeopteryx, you Hart Crane / flew where others falter" (also included in a later poem, "2 Propositions and 3 Proofs").

[129] Marsden Hartley (1877-1943), the painter, had three shows at the Walker Gallery in New York: February 28-April 2, 1938; March 6-April 8, 1939; and March 11-March 30, 1940. See also Olson's portrait of him in "Letter 7" of *The Maximus Poems* (*Maximus* I, 30-34).

[130]A statement made earlier in *Call Me Ishmael* (New York, 1947), p. 119.

[131] Josef Strzygowski (1862-1941), Austrian art historian, whose *Origins of Christian Church Art* (Oxford, 1923) discusses the influence that Northern and Iranian art had upon Western civilization.

[132] Definition from *Webster's Collegiate Dictionary*, 5th ed. (Springfield, Mass., 1945), p. 590.

[133] Pico della Mirandola as quoted in Pater (quoted earlier in Creeley's May 24 letter and in his poem "From Pico & the Women," *The Charm*, p. 14).

[134] An early version of Creeley's review of *Y & X*; different from the one Robert Payne published in *Montevallo Review*, 1 (Summer 1950), 59-60 (in *A Quick Graph*, pp. 151-53). The "poor chap" quoted in it is Olson himself.

[135] "Notes for a New Prose," published eventually in *Origin*, no. 2 (Summer 1951), 94-99 (*A Quick Graph*, pp. 11-17). Sent Olson with the following note: "O: had written this last nite, sick with cold/ etc. Sent it to Payne, an offering. What do you think? Wd you be good enough to send this back/ too beat to make a copy/ 'I am dying, Egypt, etc. . . .'" (original in Washington University Library).

[136] Olson's poem (unpublished), "IN ANSWER TO A REQUEST FOR DIRGE WORDS—THAT IS, WORDS INTENDED FOR MAKING A CATHARSIS . . . ," beginning: "The Office of the Dead is always open, at all hours / of the day & night, like a diner . . ."

[137] Williams' "The Trees" (*Complete Collected Poems*, pp. 190-91).

I. Index of Persons Named in the Letters

Printed July 1980 in Santa Barbara and Ann Arbor for the Black Sparrow Press by Mackintosh and Young & Edwards Brothers, Inc. Design by Barbara Martin. This edition is published in paper wrappers; there are 1000 hardcover trade copies; 250 hardcover copies have been numbered & signed by Robert Creeley; & 26 lettered copies have been handbound in boards by Earle Gray & are signed by George Butterick & Robert Creeley.

George F. Butterick studied with both Charles Olson and Robert Creeley at the State University of New York at Buffalo, where he received his Ph.D. in 1970. He is Curator of Literary Manuscripts and Lecturer in English at the Universtiy of Connecticut, and lives with his wife and sons in the nearby mill city of Willimantic. He is currently editing Charles Olson's unpublished prose and poetry and, more slowly, writing a biography of the poet.